ISLANDS IN THE STORM

By William Sargent

ABOUT THE AUTHOR

William Sargent is a NOVA consultant and winner of the Boston Globe's Winship award for best book by a New England author. He has written 19 books about science, nature and the environment. He is a frequent guest on National Public radio and often writes for publications like the Boston Globe and Smithsonian Magazine.

He was a research assistant at the Woods Hole Oceanographic Institution and head of the National Aquarium in Baltimore. He is presently the director of the Coastlines project in Ipswich Massachusetts and has taught science writing at Harvard University and marine biology in the Briarwood Center near Woods Hole.

PRAISE FOR WILLIAM SARGENT'S PAST BOOKS

"With his fine descriptions and lucid explanations, Sargent joins the company of Lewis Thomas and Stephen Jay Gould as a first rate interpreter of modern science." -*Publisher's Weekly*

"It is a gem of Natural History... the best introduction to the original environment of the New England coast."- *Dr. E. O. Wilson, Harvard University*

"A joy to read." -*The Washington Post*

"A Great Read! Sargent takes us on a raucous jaunt through the New England forest, to see the big picture with unclouded eyes. A true biologist he examines everything in sight and counts it relevant, connecting it with seamless prose into the rational new picture. It's a powerful boost to the new Nature religion that references us to Life on Earth." - *Dr. Bernd Heinrich*

It's science writing that reads like a novel, with all the page-turning excitement of a thriller." - *William Martin*

"Sargent can turn an event as mundane as a rising tide into poetry. This is a book for everyone who loves the shore, especially Cape Cod." - *The Boston Globe*

"If you only have time for one book about life-death dramas played to the sound of crashing waves, about new science and the old sea, about Nobel prizes, squid brains and sex orgies on Cape Cod beaches, then this book is for you."
- *Dr. A.A. Moscona, Journal of the American Medical Association*

Acknowledgements

For years I have been casually looking at Plum Island from our house in Ipswich, Massachusetts. But in 2008 a Thanksgiving storm washed Gerri Buzzotta's Plum Island home into the raging Atlantic. I wrote about the tragic incident and decided to pay closer attention to the situation.

By 2012 it became clear that something had changed on Plum Island. There was no longer enough sand being washed out of the center of the island to protect the 1200 houses to the North. The island had reached a point of no return.

I mentioned this in the Boston Globe and all hell broke lose. Everybody pretty much told me I didn't know what I was talking about. They were probably correct, so I decided to write some more. John Lockwood stepped in and helpfully offered to publish my musings in the Newburyport Current.

I also discovered that a group of local people were thinking about setting up a non-profit organization to investigate the effects of sea level rise on Greater Newburyport. With much trepidation I decided to cross that indeterminate line between observer and participant and join. After several raucous meetings they decided to call themselves the Storm Surge Coastal Adaptation Workgroup.

It was through writing for these two organizations that I started to meet more of the homeowners on Plum Island. It was not always under the best of circumstances. We had four major storms in the winter of 2012- 2013. Thirty percent of the houses in one section of Plum Island were seriously damaged.

Six houses tumbled into the sea, thirty-nine were condemned and one was moved to the other side of the street. It was one of the most concentrated areas of erosion on the East Coast.

I was with many of these people in their homes or on the beach when these events happened. It was not a good way to meet someone for the first time. But I found that throughout the ordeal the homeowners remained gracious under the most trying of times. Afterwards I grew to like them more and more as they allowed me to sit in on their emergency strategy meetings.

I would particularly like to thank, Bob and Kathy Connors, Marc Sarkady, Mark Richey, Teresa Richey, Cheryl Comeau, Tom Gorenflo, Ron Barrett, Ross Westcott, Doug Packer, Joe Storey, Tracy Blais and Dave Mountain . I hope I have told your stories well and made the right decision to write about my first impressions of you in the midst of crisis as well as during the months and year that followed.

I would also like to thank the many members of The Storm Surge group. They include Mike Morris, Elizabeth Marcus, Ron Martino, Deb Carey, John Harwood, Art Currier, Sheila Taintor, Conrad Willeman, Chris Czernik, Erika Spanger-Siegfried and so many more.

I would like to thank Geoffrey Day, Camron Abiddi, Lucy Lockwood, Peter Phippen, Nancy Pau, Bob Barker and Scott Lopreste for their excellent and delicious work with oysters and Frank Drauszewski for letting us hold our meetings and present speakers at the Parker River Wildlife Refuge. Rob Thieler was one of our first speakers and helped guide Storm Surge through its early development. It was a great delight working with Steve Manley, Casey Atkins and Joe Texeira on their various video projects.

And of course Becky Karlins for all her work and good counsel in designing this book!

Beth Aaling, Drew Marc Aurelle, Patricia Connelly and Marian Houck at The Quebec Labrador Foundation, the Newburyport Institute for Savings and the United Charities Program in Washington made all of these projects possible.

Finally I would like to thank Kristina and Chappell who put up with my many late nights spent in sometimes dangerous storms on Plum Island and my many long hours spent in our attic, writing up the results. Thank you for your love, patience, support and understanding.

TABLE OF CONTENTS

TABLE OF CONTENTS

All illustrations by William Sargent, unless otherwise noted.

ISLANDS IN THE STORM

FOREWORD

In the beginning man discovered fire and it was good. It warmed his hearth, heated his home, cooked his food and sent only tiny twists of smoke curling up through the morning's cool air.

In the Seventeen hundreds man discovered coal and it was good. It could boil water, generate steam, power engines and do the work of a million horses. Miners formed unions, the labor movement was born, but the skies grew heavy with dark clouds of smoke and invisible carbon dioxide. Cities choked, miners died and the oceans and atmosphere warmed.

In 1859 Edwin Drake drilled the first oil well oil in Titusville Pennsylvania and it was good. People could now drive cars, and fly planes. The age of mobility and freedom was born, but as man's new inventions guzzled the black gold, more carbon dioxide billowed invisibly into the atmosphere. Water and air temperatures rose and the oceans lapped ever higher on our shores.

The first of the heat-induced storms destroyed our vulnerable low-lying cities like well placed nuclear bombs. In 1992, Hurricane Andrew caused $26 billion dollars in damages in Miami and left eighty percent of the families in nearby Homestead without homes. In 2005, Hurricane Katrina killed 1833 people, destroyed 1.2 million homes and caused $108 billion dollars worth of damages in New Orleans.

In 2012, Hurricane Sandy flooded the financial capital of the world, caused $71 Billion dollars in damages, killed over 200 peo-ple and destroyed over 300, 000 homes in New York and on the Jersey Shore.

If a foreign nation had devastated three of our major cities we would know how to respond. It seems to be hard-wired into our primate genes. But how do you respond to something invisible that helped build our civilizations and accumulated slowly over the past three centuries? How do you beat back the rising seas, fight the forces of nature, defeat an invisible foe? Can we admit the enemy is really us and not some group of "other" people who want to prevent us from enjoying what we like to call our God right, the dicey proposition of living beside the restless sea?

These storms damaged islands the most severely. Key Biscayne in Florida, Chandelier and Dauphin islands off New Orleans; Staten, Manhattan and Fire islands off New York and Plum Island off New England. In this book we will visit some of these Islands in the Storm, chronicle the events that took place there and revisit them again to see how well they have prepared for the future.

Looking down on New Jersey

INTRODUCTION
REFLECTIONS OVER NEW JERSEY
February 2013

Several years ago I flew up the East Coast from Florida to Boston. It was on one of those cobalt blue days when the shore stands out starkly against the deep green of the ocean. Suddenly I realized we were flying over Atlantic City made famous by the game of Monopoly. I could almost pick out Boardwalk and Park Place, Ventnor and St Charles. I could see the utilities that supported the once thriving ocean resort and the railroads that had put it on the map.

I could also see seawalls that outlined the shore and a lattice-work of groins and jetties that poked into the Atlantic like so many toothpicks skewering a plateful of canapés. The seawalls were the real-life property owner's favorite method of preventing their expensive hotels and casinos from toppling into the Atlantic. The groins were their favorite method of trapping the sand washed away by the seawalls.

These skeletal artifacts were the remains of an era when Atlantic City reigned as the queen of American resorts, when incoming trains disgorged kings and presidents, socialites and starlets. It was the place where John Phillip Sousa sent chills up the spines of summer audiences and Jack Dempsey jogged along the beach to prepare for his bout with Gene Tunney.

But today the beach is gone, the hotels are boarded up and the city is used by coastal geologists as a textbook example of the wrong way to battle the effects of sea level rise.

From an altitude of 3,000 feet it is easy to see the folly of build-ing on a fragile barrier beach. It is easy to condemn the greed and shortsightedness of rapacious investors and the mendacious complicity of government officials.

But from 3,000 feet, it is also easy to miss the human story; to disregard the deep seated instinct to defend our property and to ignore the overwhelming sense of loss humans feel when we lose a battle to keep our homes. Each block, house, deck and boat be-low me had witnessed human stories. Some people had won brief battles with the ocean; others had endured tragedies, that would reverberate through their families for generations.

It was to investigate these kinds of stories that I spent several years talking to the inhabitants of Plum Island, Massachusetts and other barrier beach islands devastated by hurricane Sandy. I spoke with homeowners, lawyers, politicians and scientists as they struggled to come to grips with the effect of sea level rise – considered to be the fastest racehorse in the oncoming environ-mental apocalypse.

Their stories had protagonists, antagonists, drama and action. I talked to hundreds of people facing the prospect of losing their homes, their jobs and their livelihoods. I've seen them make good choices and bad, wise decisions and dumb ones.

During these encounters I grew to like the people involved and appreciated their spirit and political acumen. I grew less enamored of the callousness of those who put all the blame on the home-owners. We are all to blame for a system that has encouraged people to live on the coasts for the past 200 years.

I have tried to tell the story through the eyes of the people in-volved. I have also relied on newspaper articles, scientific papers and official papers to complement their memories of past events. I apologize to some of my informants who had to put up with my innumerable phone calls.

Of the hundreds of stories I could have used I selected only a few that I hope will be representative of the whole. Another writer might have selected other stories and written an entirely different book. But I hope the story I have told captures the essence of the human drama and the science and law surrounding the incidents on Plum Island and around the world.

I was fortunate that the story of Plum Island spanned the time both before, during and after hurricane Sandy. By the end of 2012 Plum Island had tried just about every hard core engineering solution and none of them had worked. Sandy made it clear that if we want to continue living on the coast we have to learn how to work with nature not fight against it. I believe there is cause for great optimism in this new mindset. Climate change is making us appreciate the recurrent resilience and beauty of nature.

Finally, I must add a personal note that undoubtedly has some bearing on this book. I grew up in a house that overlooks Cape Cod's Pleasant Bay. Today I live in a house that is a quarter mile inland. Many people might consider that I still live on the water, but I know I do not. Most days I never even see the ocean. Anyone who has ever had the privilege of living on the water knows how different it is from being an inlander—one is like visiting Paris, the other like being Parisian.

When you live on the water, the moods of the ocean shape your life. You feel the power of nature when an Atlantic Storm pounds the shore. You marvel at the ocean's beauty when her waters reflect a shimmering trail of moonlight on a quiet evening in June. You alter your day's activities after seeing seals on a rock or terns working over bait fish at dawn.

There is a world of difference between living on the water and going to the beach. The first gives you an abiding sense of place; the other, a pleasant afternoon.

I would not be writing the books I am writing today, if I had not grown up on the water. Could Thoreau have written Walden from downtown Concord or Henry Beston written the Outermost House from Eastham Center? Living on the water launched my career and stamped its imprint on my life forever. If that experience has shaped this book, I acknowledge it, without hesitation, as a stated bias.

Local officials surveying Geri Buzzotta's lot.

CHAPTER I
GERI'S LOSS
November 25, 2008

On November 25, 2008, Geri Buzzotta put away the baked goods she had been making for Thanksgiving morning, said goodnight to the picture of her deceased husband Mario, and fell into a fitful sleep. An hour later her grandson heard a crack in the floor below his bed and rushed to his grandmother's side.

"Grandma what was that noise?"

"Oh, you probably just heard an especially big wave. This house has weathered many a storm, now just go back to bed. Tomorrow is going to be a big day."

"No Grandma, I heard it right under my feet. I think we need to get out of here!"

Another crack and Geri was convinced, she left her house of 46 years with only her grandson, her pet Chihuahua Oliver, and the nightgown she was wearing.

When she returned the next morning Geri was blocked from returning to her house. Her lot was cordoned off with yellow tape, and a cluster of town officials mingled beside her front door. The building inspector, Sam Joslin, broke away from the group to tell her she couldn't go back into her own home.

"But Sam, I need to some clothes and the cookies I made for Thanksgiving! My only picture of Mario is in there too!"

"I'm sorry Geri, I cant let anyone back inside. The central support beam under your house has broken.

Several hours later Joslin gave the word and an excavator nudged Geri's house gently over the dune's edge and pieces of her former home tumbled into the frigid waters of the Atlantic Ocean.

"I'm sorry Geri," said Sam turning to hug his neighbor.
"Sam, I thank you honey. It wasn't your fault. I just wonder if Mario is looking down."

Mario Buzzotta had bought the converted shack for Geri 43 years before. Then, with their own hands, they had lovingly remodeled it into their ocean front dream house. But, now Geri's savings, her belongings and Mario were all gone. The house had been all she had really wanted and now it too was washing back and forth in the incoming waves.

Geri's loss was just the most recent chapter in a long story of Plum Island woes. The island is an eleven-mile long barrier beach situated near the New Hampshire border. It is jointly owned by the towns of Newbury, Newburyport, Rowley, Ipswich, The Parker River Wildlife Refuge and the Commonwealth of Massachusetts.

Plum Island was first mapped in 1616 by Captain John Smith, and named for the succulent beach plums that proliferated in its dunes. Like most East Coast barrier beaches, Plum Island has long been used by vacationers. During the late 19th Century large hotels serviced the island's summer visitors.

But, like most East Coast barrier beaches Plum Island is also eroding. The reason is sea level rise. Storms in the '40's, '50's, 60's '70's, 80's and 90's swept dozens of cottages off the beach. By 1952, The Army Corps of Engineers had already declared the island in imminent danger of breaking in two. Mrs. Buzzotta's 2008 tragedy was only the beginning of the most recent phase of rapid erosion.

With such a history, you would think that officials would have tried to discourage development on the fragile island. Instead, the EPA urged the communities of Newbury and Newburyport to spend $30 Million dollars in 2004 to bury municipal water and sewer lines in the dunes running the length of the island. If a new inlet forms, as could be expected in any major storm, up to 750 winterized homes could be cut off from water, sewerage and rescue vehicles.

But Geri's loss also spurred local officials to complete a story-high seawall of sand-filled jute sandbags. The idea behind the $2.5 Million dollar project was to provide time so the Army Corps of Engineers could come in and devise a more permanent solution to the island's woes.

But is there a permanent solution? Plum Island is made possible by the erosion of the large dunes in the center of the island. As the dunes erode, currents sweep sand both south to build up Crane's Beach in Ipswich and north to protect the homes of north Plum Island. Sand also travels down the nearby Merrimack River to accumulate on offshore sandbars that help protect the beach from Northeast storms. Today, most of the town's focus is centered on having the Army Corps of Engineers repair the jetties at the mouth of the Merrimack River, and using dredged sand from the river to stabilize the beach.

However, the real problem is that the sea is rising and that the dunes in the center of the island are running out of sand. What sand does come off the dunes is blocked by groins from reaching the area where the island is most likely to break in two. One solution would be to remove or modify these groins. The other solution would be to retreat from this fragile North Atlantic redoubt and gradually incorporate it into the existing Plum Island Wildlife Refuge.

As in so many cases like this, the town of Newbury is doing exactly the wrong thing. It owns five and a half acres of primary and secondary dunes immediately adjacent to the Refuge. But instead of deeding the lot to the Refuge, the cash strapped town tried to sell the lot to a developer so he can build a house in the fragile dunes.

It is a meshugena idea, made all the more crazy because the lot provided the sand that flows north to protect the island's older homes. Sure, the town would have received a few more years worth of taxes if the proposal had gone through, but in two to five years the new houses would have also been hanging over the edge and the older houses long gone. It would not have been the end of the world, but the losses would have reverberated through all the families for generations to come. That is the true cost of sea level rise and it is one that can be prevented by gradually allowing these fragile areas to revert back to nature.

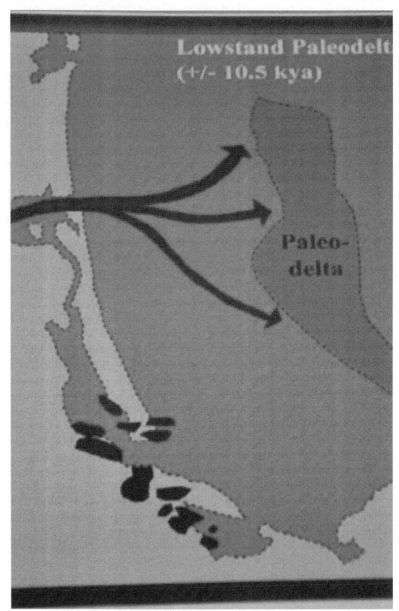

Plum Island 10,000 years ago.
Courtesy Mike Morris

CHAPTER 2
PLUM ISLAND
10,000 Years Ago

Plum Island is one of 200 barrier beach islands that stretch along the East Coast from New England to Florida and along the Gulf of Mexico to Padre Island, Texas. They make up the longest barrier beach system on our planet and are natural breakwaters, crucial to protecting over a million people from the ravages of sea level rise.

The sand that makes up these beaches has been forming for millions of years. It comes from the gradual breakdown of the craggy mountains of New England, the gentle foothills of the Mid-Atlantic Piedmont and from the shells of billions of mollusks, coral and curious shell covered bacteria that thrive off our southern coasts.

The best way to understand how Plum Island formed is to go back to the last Ice Age. A mile thick glacier had been grinding over the mountains of New Hampshire and Maine pulverizing their granite cores into tiny almost indestructible grains of minerals; silica, magnetite, mica, even minute gems of semi-precious red garnet. These tumbled down the sides of mountains, and collected in meltwater streams.

The ocean was still 250 feet lower than today and the coast was almost 5 miles further to the East, but about eighteen thousand years ago the world started emerging from the ice ages. The seas were rising almost three feet every fifty years, or about six times faster than at today's pace.

In places the seas were rising so fast that sixty feet of land would be inundated in a single year. Florida sank to half its former size, and most of the events that left places like coastal New England in their present form happened in less than a thousand years.

The second way to understand how Plum Island formed is to drive to Franconia New Hampshire on a nice hot summer's day and float on your back in Echo Lake. Less than ten years ago you would have been under the watchful eyes of the Old Man of the Mountain, today you might see bear cubs gamboling about in the meadowed flanks of Cannon Mountain, seemingly just above your head.

It is erosion of these mountains that continues to make Plum Island possible. But how do the grains of minerals get transported to the coast? The answer lies at both ends of Echo Lake. A rivulet of crystal clear water seeps out of the west side of the lake to become the Connecticut River and another stream trickles out of the boggy east side of the lake to become the Pemigewasset River and later the Merrimack River that flows into the Atlantic Ocean between Salisbury Beach and Plum Island.

The mouth of the river was still almost 5 miles east of its present location, but the climate was starting to stabilize so the river that emerged from beneath the glacier braided into myriads of meltwater streams that built up a broad delta of sand.

Then waves and currents started to reshape this sand into a long thin barrier beach about half a mile seaward of the mainland. About five thousand years ago the rate of sea level rise slowed to its present rate of about a foot every hundred years. But that was more than enough to cause Proto Plum Island to retreat between two feet to ten feet every year depending on the strength of storms.

Because waves tended to come in from the east they piled up water along the front of the island and it had to go somewhere so it formed longshore currents that carried sand from the reservoir of Paleolithic sand at the center of the island south toward present day Ipswich and north toward the Merrimack River.

The other thing that happened is that the island started to move through a process that geologists call rollover. This can occur gradually every day when the onshore wind blows dry sand off the beach into the dunes, but it can also happen dramatically when a storm washes as much as 60 feet of sand off the front of an island and deposits it on the backside of the island. In essence, the island rolls over itself migrating toward the mainland, which is itself migrating westward through gradual erosion.

If you were to take a time-lapse photo of Plum Island you would see that it constantly moves, shifts and pulsates like a living organism. As long as it is free to move it can build and repair itself after every storm. But if you put an immovable structure on such a beach, the beach can no longer act as a moveable barrier to protect the mainland from the effects of sea level rise.

This process has been going on for over ten thousand year and for about nine thousands and five hundred of those years humans have been content to just visit barrier beaches like Plum Island for food and respite. It has only been in the last hundred years that humans have had the temerity to think they could actually build permanent structures even cities on such fragile stretches of ever moving sand. This has made losses like those of Geri Buzzotta's in 2008 more frequent and more devastating. This then will be the story of people trying to live and survive on these islands in the storm.

A Plum Island Home

"The Most Dangerous River Mouth on the East Coast. "
- U.S. Coast Guard

CHAPTER 3
THE MERRIMACK RIVER
August 8, 2013

The developed part of Plum Island stands astride two towns, Newburyport and Newbury on the northern coast of Massachusetts. The towns voted to break apart in 1764 because Newbury had stayed rural, poor and agricultural while Newburyport had grown rich and fat on her maritime trade.

When Newburyport seceded she was the smallest town in Massachusetts geographically, but she soon became one of the richest and was incorporated as a city in 1851. She was so prosperous that she was even in the running to become the capitol of Massachusetts but lost out because the Merrimack River, which is the source of her wealth, is also her greatest liability.

The river moved back and forth every year and silted up after major storms. Ocean-going schooners had to wait for high tide so they could just make it over the sandbar that blocked the mouth of the fast flowing river.

The entrance of the river was so dangerous that the Coast Guard is said to have been born in Newburyport because the United States built the Plum Island Station 3 miles from the center of town. However, there is some dispute, about whether the station was built more to save lives, or to save money. Newburyport sailors have always been adept at evading the authorities, first the British blockaders then U.S. revenue cutters. Apparently the town fathers had looked the other way when their neighbors dumped hundreds of pounds of tea into Newburyport Harbor, way before Boston had ever thought of holding her tea party.

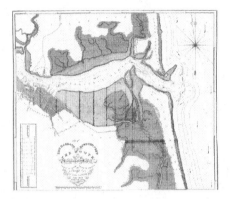

This 1826 chart shows the location of the old mouth of the Merrimack River. *Courtesy Mike Morris*

However, there is little doubt that Newburyport owed its initial burst of prosperity to her fleet of privateers that raided British ships both during the revolution and the war of 1812. The port grew richer still, making rum and importing slaves for the triangle trade, and then became even richer smuggling opium in the China Trade and hooch during Prohibition.

The city redeemed itself, somewhat, by producing the writer John Marquand and the abolitionist William Lloyd Garrison and it is said that more than a few of her stately homes became way stations in the underground railway. But the port maintained its flair for eccentric characters in the personage of Lord Timothy Dexter who is the only person in history to have actually shipped coals to Newcastle.

Dexter was the laughing stock of Newburyport until his ships arrived in Newcastle and found that British miners had just gone on strike. There was a desperate need for fuel and Dexter made a killing selling the city's merchants good old American coal. Of course he had made his first fortune by selling gold to buy up Continental dollars that were almost worthless during the revolution but became priceless after the war was won—some fool he!

But all the fun ended for Newburyport in the 1950's when strip malls and highways drew shoppers away from her old rundown commercial center. The town fathers wanted to raze the entire area but changed their minds at the last minute and applied for a federal grant to restore and renovate the city's historic buildings in 1970. Today Newburyport remains as one of our nation's foremost examples of how to preserve a city through restoration and renovation.

The best way to learn about a riverside city like Newburyport is to see it by boat. This transports you back in time to when the Carr family used to ferry stagecoaches from the Portsmouth Flying Stage Coach Company across the Merrimack River so the coaches could complete their run from Boston to New Hampshire. You can see the stone sidings where lumberjacks used to crib up hundreds of logs floated downstream from Maine and New Hampshire to be used in shipbuilding.

Many of the logs would be guided down Plum Island Sound and through the Fox Creek canal, cut so narrowly into the Ipswich marshes that only a single log could fit through the creek at one time. In Essex the logs would be fashioned into fishing smacks to ply the waters of Georges Bank. But the best timber would be saved for Newburyport's own shipbuilding.

You also notice that Newburyport is a shadow of her former self. The banks of the Merrimack River used to be covered with boat yards, rope works and iron forges. This was where Donald McKay started building his world famous McKay Clippers, that still hold records for fastest passages to places like Europe, the Orient and the gold fields of San Francisco. So many ships had the name Newburyport painted on their sternmost escutcheons that people in China thought that Newburyport was its own country.

The Merrimack Arms Company made derringer pistols in the mid-1800's and the harbor was jammed with schooners carrying coal bound for the textile mills in Lowell and Lawrence. Barges and tugboats used to transport the coal upriver from a massive offloading platform in Newburyport harbor, but when the mills started replacing coal with diesel it doomed the river's last major commercial activity to oblivion.

Today, thousands of pleasure craft moor where tall ships once set out for the Orient and an extensive marsh has grown over the former shipyards. Osprey poles jut out here and there up through marsh. Some of them have cameras attached so you can go home and watch the chicks hatch on your computer. Bald eagles like to rest on these camera housings when they fly down the river to hunt for fish during the winter when the river stays open even during the coldest months. It is a chilly reminder that August will soon be over and we will be in the peak of the hurricane season.

The Merrimack River

The Weather Channel on Plum Island

CHAPTER 4
SEA LEVEL RISE
October 15, 2012

In early September a Boston television station asked me if I would do an interview about erosion on Plum Island. I agreed but it didn't make much sense. True, Hurricane Leslie was churning up the coast, but it was well offshore. It would raise some "awesome surf," but it was doubtful it would erode any Plum Island homes.

When I arrived at the beach, I started to understand the situation. Several homeowners to the south of Gerri Buzzotta's abandoned lot were trying to get permission to use bulldozers to scrap sand off the beach and push it up against the dunes supporting their homes.

Erosion is an ongoing issue that is getting worse as the sea level rises. In the ten short years we have lived on the North Shore, several Plum Island homes have been abandoned, one has been moved back 20 feet and the Buzzzotta home toppled into the Atlantic Ocean.

The situation is the same all over coastal Massachusetts. The Cape Cod National Seashore had had to demolish its five threatened Chatham camps in March 2012, and private homes had been moved back from the coast on Martha's Vineyard and Nantucket a few years before. Every time a storm approaches some poor rain sodden journalist has to go stand in front of the same jeopardized South Shore house they covered the year before. They have become old friends with the homeowners they see during every storm.

It was clear that the homeowners were using the distant threat of the hurricane to garner sympathy to get permission to scrape the beach. It was doubtful that simply pushing some sand around was going to make much difference, but it is important that people feel they can do something to protect their homes even when the outcome is inevitable.

The Boston Globe called a few weeks later. They wanted to do an article about the scrapping itself. I told the reporter that I didn't like to be the person who had to say it but the scraping probably wasn't going to work. Then I didn't hear anything for several weeks and figured the Globe had probably dropped the article in favor of more important stories.

When the article finally did appear I realized they had been waiting for the scrapping decision to be made. I was just as happy. I doubted that my interview would have made a difference but I also didn't want to think that it might have effected the final decision. As long as the homeowners were willing to foot the bill themselves, I felt that it was important for them to feel they had put up a good fight.

But the article raised a furor. One homeowner said I should get my head out a textbook and go out and see the real world. I wish some of my former professors could have seen that quote! Another homeowner said I overlooked the absolute right of private property and that it was impossible to reverse 300 years of development. I think the homeowners missed the point that it was the ocean not me that had no regard for the absolute right of private property or the rules promulgated by humans. It is the laws of nature that will supersede the so-called rights of mankind.

When the scraping was finally finished it left a beach unlike any I had ever seen before. Bulldozers were running up and down a long slope of sand that stretched from the ocean to the houses above. It was totally unlike the contours of a beach shaped by the forces of nature with a berm, a platform and dunes. It looked like some parents had told their children it was time to leave the beach so they had simply dumped a final bucket of sand in front of their sand castle and left for the night.

But the October tides were going to be the highest of the year. It was clear that the beach was going to be just fine it would quickly return to its natural contours. It was the immovable homes on dunes that needed to move that would soon be in trouble.

CHAPTER 5
SUPERSTORM SANDY
NY October 29, 2012

Michael Abbruzzo was shocked to see George Dresch still sitting in his house the day before the storm. "Dude, why don't you go? What's the point? I got the wife and girls out last night."

George didn't have to say much. They both remembered the year before when their homes had both been burglarized when they had evacuated for Hurricane Irene. Perhaps that is why George decided to stay in the face of Superstorm Sandy.

He must have regretted it all night long as huge waves broke over his Staten Island home. The following morning all that Michael could find was a big gaping hole where George and his family had once lived.

Rescuers found the remains of twelve-year old Angela Dresch a block away from their former home, then found her mother who was still breathing amidst the debris.

They found the battered body of George Dresch, sandwiched between two nearby homes. Had he tried to go for help, or simply been swept out of his home by a massive wave?

Michael was in shock. He had always liked George; his family had taken care of the Abruzzo's dog when they went on vacation. Now the Dresches were gone and his neighborhood was in smithereens.

Over a hundred other people died that night for a hundred different reasons. One eight-year old boy was crushed by a tree when he ran outside to check on his family's calves A Pennsylvania woman died when she skidded off a snowy road, another woman was electrocuted by a downed electric wire, and another had washed up on Georgia Beach in the Hamptons.

Three people were found drowned in their basements in the far Rockaways and a 75 year-old woman died from a heart attack after the power blinked out on her respirator. Several more people died walking their dogs and two boys were crushed while they were doing what they were supposed be doing, staying home and watching TV.

Sandy had been a strange storm from her inception. The crew of a hurricane hunter plane had discovered her as a long low tropical depression hanging almost stationary over the hot waters of the Caribbean. Hanging over eighty degree waters was not a good sign at this time of year. Normally such late forming storms were created off of Africa and traveled across the Atlantic before grazing the East Coast and heading back out to sea. Not this one.

On October 24th, NOAA declared Sandy a Category 1 hurricane just before she slammed into Jamaica, Cuba and the Bahamas killing 69 people. But then something started to puzzle the meteorologists. The ensemble models they used to make forecasts looked like pieces of spaghetti spewing out all over the map.

Half of Sandy's tracks were leading her safely out to sea as the forecasters expected. But the two most reliable models had her making a sharp left turn before whacking the East Coast near New Jersey. But then, day after day the other squiggles started to line up together over the highly unusual late season track. This finally gave forecasters the confidence that their models were right. It was a highly unusual track but it was also strikingly close to the track taken by Irene the year before. She had been a billion dollar storm that had tracked inland devastating a huge swath of land from the coast and up through Vermont and into Canada. Was this going to be the new normal, a hundred year storm every season?

Meanwhile Sandy's winds dropped as she veered offshore as expected. But she was busy incorporating the energy of a cold front that had been blocking her passage west. She was becoming a hybrid storm, a Northeaster with a warm tropical core packing hurricane force winds.

But Sandy was deceptive. She lurked several hundred miles offshore as a category I hurricane moving slowly northward. You could watch as she lashed the coasts of Florida and the Carolinas but it didn't look nearly as bad as what the forecasters had started calling a historic Frankenstorm. She even dropped back down to a tropical storm before turning left and slamming into Atlantic City two days before Halloween.

The East Coast woke up to a changed world. New York City was devastated. Hundreds of illegally parked cars were underwater in lower Manhattan. The subway tunnels to New Jersey and Brooklyn were flooded. It would take five days to pump them out and at least a week to get the trains running again. A hundred houses were burning in Queens, the side of a building had collapsed during the night in Chelsea leaving the front side exposed like the open end of a doll's house. A huge crane had collapsed during the night and was dangling ominously over East 57th Street. Wall Street would be closed for two consecutive days, the first time since the blizzard on 1888.

Millions of people were without water and electricity. Nobody could work, there was no transportation. You couldn't get any money because all the ATM machines were down. Even food became a problem for yuppies because most New York restaurants stored their food in freezers in their basement which were now flooded under several feet of fetid water. Just to add a Hollywood twist, the Captain of the ship used to make the film Pirates of the Caribbean had gone down with his ship when it came apart in the storm off the Carolinas. One of her last ports of call had been Newburyport because one of crew members had come from the area.

The situation was even worse in New Jersey where the hybrid storm had made landfall. Her entire coast of fragile barrier beach communities had been destroyed, but the destruction was so great it would take almost a week to be able to assess the full extent of the damage.

It didn't take long for political pundits to start weighing in about whether Sandy had been caused by global warming. It was less than a week before the national election and both candidates had avoided mentioning global warming like the plague. But you can only ignore Mother Nature for so long. Forget anything that Donald Trump had to offer. Sandy was the real October surprise.

October Phragmites

CHAPTER 6
COASTAL TRIAGE
October 30, 2012

On October 30th the United States awoke up to a new reality. Another city had been devastated by a major storm and all of New Jersey's barrier beach communities were now underwater.

It was the third time in the last twenty years that this has happened. First it was Miami in 1995, then New Orleans in 2005, and now New York in 2012. It is clear that we are in a new climatic regime of more frequent major storms, though it is important to point out that none of these storms were over a Category 3.

We had to now make decisions about which cities and towns we could afford to save and protect in the face of rising seas and more frequent storms. The decision was easy for New York. It was America's most populous city and the financial capital of the world. It was also built on a platform of Palisades bedrock though too many of its subways and tunnels were built below the height of the ocean.

Governor Cuomo was already discussing the idea of building a storm surge barrier similar to the one that protects London. It would cost at least $10 Billion and take several years to complete, but in the infelicitous words of our time, New York was simply too big and too important to fail. I could do without two of their sports stadiums but that is a topic for a different time and place.

But what about the barrier beach communities of the beautiful Jersey Shore? There were built on narrow strips of sand only a few feet above sea level. Barrier beaches must be able to move, to stay healthy. They do this everyday, but we only become aware of it after a major storm when hundreds of feet of sand have been eroded off the front of the beach, washed over the island and been deposited in the shallow bay behind. The beach has essentially migrated several hundred feet closer to the mainland where it will reform so it can continue to function as a living barrier to protect the mainland from the next storm.

But neither of these things can happen if you build immovable structures like buildings, boardwalks, groins and seawalls on a barrier beach that is only twenty blocks wide. We saw the results as the ocean washed through the streets of Atlantic City. Now it is our turn to make some astute decisions about whether to sell Boardwalk or Park Place.

The owners of the homes and hotels, and the State of New Jersey would soon be eligible to receive two kinds of FEMA grants. Mitigation grants would provide homeowners with tax-supported money to rebuild their buildings on the same location as before and acquisition grants that would provide the New Jersey with funds to pay homeowners the fair market price for their buildings. Under the terms of the agreement, the state must then convert the land into green areas that would allow the beaches to be able to move as nature intended.

The private owner could use his buyout money to do whatever he wanted to do, whether it be sending his kids to college or moving to higher ground. But the amount of money designated for this "experimental" buyout program was much smaller than the amount of money designated for rebuilding.

Hopefully both the President and Congress would heed the lessons of Sandy and replenish the pot designated for buyouts. It was a common sense, permanent solution that both Democrats and Republicans should be able to support.

CHAPTER 7
CATALYST FOR CHANGE?
October 30, 2012

It took awhile to figure out what happened in New Jersey. Unlike New York City that sits on average about 45 feet about sea level and rises as high as 250 feet above the ocean on the Palisades, the entire coast of New Jersey is made up of towns and cities perched on low lying strips of sand less than twenty feet above high tide.

Twenty-foot waves had simply washed over the entire 127-mile long coast destroying amusement parks, boardwalks, hotels, homes and casinos. It burst through several of the beaches cutting off hundreds of thousands of people in flooded homes without food, water or electricity. They were only too happy to see the reassuring uniforms of the National Guard troops that rescued them from their homes the day after the storm.

The entire scene was in marked contrast to what had happened after Katrina and Hurricane Andrew. President Obama had been determined to get it right from when he entered office. He had removed the political hacks that always seem to be appointed to FEMA under Republican presidents. Their rescuers had fanned out after the storm providing water, food, fuel and housing. It was reassuring to see such a well-organized response.

But people noticed something else the day after the storm. The ocean had torn almost a thousand feet off the front of the barrier beaches and washed tons of sand over and islands burying streets and homes. They were in the process of rolling over as coastal geologists said they would.

The same thing happened fifty years before during the Ash Wednesday storm of 1962.

The Ash Wednesday storm was not a hurricane but it proved to be a catalyst for our present day understanding of barrier beach dynamics. The rogue storm arrived on a moonless night in March then raged up and down a thousand miles of coast for three more days. It struck when the moon was closest to the earth and the sun and the moon were aligned. These astronomical conditions produced the feared Perigean spring tides that only occur every two years.

The storm also struck after winter storms had already removed much of the beaches' protective sands and it continued through five cycles of maximum high tide erosion. It was the worst possible storm occurring at the worst possible time.

The storm devastated the coasts from Florida to Cape Cod, but slammed into New Jersey particularly hard. Thirty-foot waves crumpled Atlantic City's famous steel pier and splintered Ocean City's boardwalk. Fortyfive thousand beachfront homes tumbled into the Atlantic in New Jersey alone. Coastal dwellers were stunned by the damage. Scores of inlets had slashed through barrier beaches and the dunes had been all but flattened.

Such storms are not known for killing people. But this one had killed 32 people and caused half a billion dollars in damages. Perhaps it stood out particularly clearly in people's minds precisely because it occurred in an era of fewer hurricanes when people were less accustomed to experiencing major storms. Today the sea level is almost nine inches higher than it was in 1962, so Sandy crashed almost a thousand feet further inland.

But coastal geologists noticed something particularly interesting after the Ash Wednesday storm. The islands that didn't have any buildings had been able to slough off the worst effects of the storm and after a few weeks were already starting to recover.

That summer, waves pushed the displaced sand back onto the islands from the offshore bars and filled in most of the new inlets. By autumn, beach grass had re-vegetated the most eroded areas of the beach and the dunes had started to reform. Officials were so impressed with the resiliency of the natural system in Virginia, that they canceled plans to build 45,000 private beach homes and created the Assateague National Seashore instead.

The Ash Wednesday Storm had arrived at a crucial moment in America's evolving conservation ethic. In September 1962, Rachel Carson ushered in the modern environmental movement with the publication of her blockbuster *Silent Spring*. The book not only indicted the pesticide industry, it also questioned the bedrock of America's long standing belief in the traditional concept of progress, the idea that technology and money should be used to fight and defeat nature.

Yet the battered beaches of New Jersey showed that something was wrong with that traditional ethic. All the expensive groins, jetties and seawalls had not prevented the damage. In fact, like pesticides, they seemed to have made the situation worse. Yet nobody knew exactly why that was so. Here was a stable beach. You should have been able to armor it with seawalls to prevent erosion. What was wrong? Three years later we started to find some answers to the question when James Keeling published a paper that showed that carbon dioxide had risen precipitously ever year since atmospheric scientists had started measuring it in 1957. It was clear from the data that increased carbon dioxide would lead to global warming, and global warming would lead to more coastal erosion and faster sea level rise.

Keeling's data also challenged coastal geologists old concept of erosion. Traditionally they had assumed that barrier islands formed several thousand years ago in approximately the same place you find them today, so it made sense to try to stop them from eroding. Operating under that old paradigm, the Civilian Conservation Corps built a hundred mile long sand dune along the North Carolina's Outer Banks islands during the Depression. But by the 1960s the National Park Service noticed that the islands were eroding on both their front and back sides. It made sense that the ocean would erode the front of the islands, but why was the back of the islands receding as well?

It is rumored among coastal geologists that it was an inebriated old Outer Banks hermit who first came up with the answer. He kept showing up at public meetings insisting that the islands were not eroding, just migrating. Almost everyone laughed at his silly rantings but the notion still niggled at the back of some scientific minds.

Eventually the National Park Service sent a young graduate student into the field to investigate. Paul Godfrey discovered that storms normally wash sand off the front of barrier islands and deposit it on their backside marshes in the process called rollover. But the artificial sand dune was so high it was preventing sand from washing over the island so the backside marshes and beaches were receding from lack of sand.

The town crank was right, barrier islands do migrate by rolling over, and anything you do to prevent that process is doomed to failure. But islands only migrate episodically during storms, so it is easy to ignore the long-term pattern of inevitable migration, especially if you are a developer intent building beachfront homes.

Coastal geologists now realize that most of the East and Gulf Coast barrier islands formed on the edge of the continental shelves and have migrated to their present positions as the sea levels have risen since the last Ice Age. In fact the beaches, dunes, sandbars and mainland all migrate across the continental shelf as part of an integrated system. The Outer Banks have migrated as much as fifty miles and many Gulf Coast islands have migrated more than a hundred miles toward the shore. Some islands off Mississippi have migrated more than a hundred miles in the past century alone. This new realization pitted coastal geologists against homeowners, and their engineers who wanted to see each storm as an individual episode rather than an ongoing process.

Coastal geologists finally codified their new thinking in the second Skidaway Statement. But the report landed on Ronald Reagan's desk with a resounding thud. The new president was in the process of ushering in his personal era of genial, head-in-the sand anti-environmentalism.

Developers were able to dismiss the Skidaway School of coastal geologists as a bunch of Cassandras who loved public beaches but had no concern for the lives of the people they wished to remove from the coasts. As the most articulate and visible environmentalist Al Gore was eventually on the receiving end of the worst of the frat house vitriol. His mentor Roger Revelle had been a prime mover behind Keeling's original research on climate

change. So, like global warming itself, most of the science behind sea level rise had been done over forty years ago, then was
promptly ignored by public policy makers. Today we know that
the sea is rising at least 6 inches every fifty years and that this
translates into a 100 to a 1,000 foot horizontal retreat. This rate of
sea level rise will undoubtedly increase dramatically in the years
ahead. Yet communities continue to develop the coasts as if sea
level rise does not exist, and that barrier islands are stable entities
instead of moving features on our rapidly changing planet. But,
would Sandy, coming on the heels of the hottest year on record,
finally be the catalyst that would change people's minds about
coastal development?

After the Storm
Courtesy of A.P.

CHAPTER 8
THE BLIZZARD OF 2013
March 10, 2013

Priscilla Arena was desperate. It was getting cold and dark in her car, stuck in a snow bank in Farmingdale, New York. Why hadn't she left work earlier to drive home to her family? She could see their faces hovering overhead. The vision made her start crying all over again.

"No, no, I have to compose myself. My hands will soon be too cold to hold a pencil."
"God, please give me the strength to write one last letter."

She ripped a piece of paper out of her loose-leaf binder and started to write in her girlish scrawl.

"Dear John and Julia,
Remember all the things that mommy taught you... Never say you hate someone you love.... Take pride in the things you do and especially in your family... Don't get angry at the small things; it's a waste of precious time... Realize that all people are different but most are good. My love for you will never die, remember me always."

Twelve hours later a National Guard trooper saw the frosted glass on her windshield. He woke and tenderly helped her climb into the warmth of the canvas covered Army truck idling quietly beside the road. Only then could she break down into tears. She would see her family once again.

Mandatory ban on driving.

Driving Ban

Salisbury, MA

Further north the governors of Massachusetts, Rhode Island and Connecticut had declared mandatory driving bans. The punishment for not obeying these laws was a year in prison and a $500 fine. It was an unprecedented response to what the weather forecasters were now calling a historic storm.

Ed and Nancy Bemis had just finished breakfast in their small home overlooking Salisbury Beach in Massachusetts. They had made it through another sleepless night of raging winds and crashing surf. Now it was Saturday morning and they thought the worst was over. Ed started videotaping dark gray water rushing under his neighbor's house when the monstrous wave crashed through their sliding glass door.

Riding on top of the new moon high tide and four foot storm surge the wave swept all their belongings into a jumbled wet ball of lamps, chairs, books and sodden rugs, against the back wall of their living room. Nancy was pinned under the glass door with two and a half feet of muddy colored water on top of her.

Ed tried to pull off the door but it was too heavy. The next wave could sweep her back out of the house into the Atlantic Ocean's deadly grasp. But she was drowning in the seawater and sand below the glass door when their sixteen-year-old daughter ran in.

"What's going on? Mother are you alright? Help. Help!!"

Suddenly they heard a loud bang on the back door and a fireman pulled the sliding glass window off the choking woman.

"This is a code red evacuation order. Grab what you can and get into the van out back. It will take you to the shelter on Lafayette Road. "

Outside, the Bemises saw one of their neighbors clamber out of a window and into the waiting bucket of a front-end loader where he huddled up beside four other people that had escaped the freezing cold, waist deep water.

Robin Weisenstein was at the front desk of Salisbury's Ocean Front Motel when she received the mandatory evacuation call. It was 9 am. She quickly dialed all the units in the small motel before waking up her son and grandchildren.

The boiler was making a horrible noise and the acrid smell of smoke and fuel filled the tiny lobby. The roar of the surf was ominous and sepulchral.

" We've got to get out of here! Grab some clothes!!"

Robin thought the four-foot drifts of frozen snow would stop the waves but when she opened the door, they were already crashing over the dunes and flowing like the Mekong River through the second floor units. It was like a flash back, scary as hell.

She slammed the front door and pushed her grandchildren toward the back door where a fireman stood standing with an axe. Robin passed her grandchildren over the fence to the fireman who pulled them down to safety. The roar of the ocean still echoed in her ears. They had left the motel just in time.

Outside the streets were clogged with a foot-thick slurry of heavy wet sand. At first Robin thought it was from a snow truck, then she realized the waves had washed several feet of sand into the streets of the small city. Now the sand grabbed at the wheels of the van making it almost impossible to steer. It looked like they were driving through the aftermath of a muddy war.

At the evacuation shelter Robin pondered her fate. She only had ten dollars in her banking account and nowhere to go once she had to leave the shelter. Most of the other residents were in the same boat. They had all been homeless before the state placed them in Mike's Ocean Front Motel. Now they could be back out on the frozen streets for the rest of the winter. But her son and grandchildren were safe and sound beside her .

Moving Out

CHAPTER 9
AN UNNECESSARY TRAGEDY
March 2, 2013

It took me several trips to Plum Island to realize what I thought the final chapter for this saga would be. After Hurricane Sandy, beach scrapping and the February Blizzards the owners of the five damaged homes on Annapolis Way hired contractors to start building a massive seawall of sand-filled jute geotubes.

Geotubes

The contractors filled the tubes with sand until they were about four feet in diameter and then stacked them three layers deep. The final sandbag seawall was about a tenth of a mile long. By early March I realized that the sandbag seawall was already changing the profile of the beach. Now, instead of dissipating their energy by running up a long naturally sloping beach, the waves were bouncing off the face of the sandbag seawall and their un-dissipated energy was scouring out the beach below the wall.

Last summer there had been a nice broad beach below the houses where hundreds of people surfed, had picnics and walked their dogs. It was clear that this summer there would hardly be any beach left. The public would be relegated to sitting on a narrow strip of sand squeezed between low tide and the face of the sand tube seawall.

It was already a dangerous situation. We watched one man scamper up the seawall just before being swept away by an incoming wave. In the summer it could a young family sitting on the strip of sand and one of their children being swept out to sea and caught in the undertow.

The beach was so narrow that people already had to walk on the sandbags, which presented its own set of problems. We watched a homeowner try to stop an onlooker from walking on the sandbag seawall because it was protecting private property. But it was the sandbags that had made it too dangerous to walk on what was left of the beach.

But the owner had a point. Jute is a natural fiber designed to disintegrate when it is exposed to wear and tear. If too many people walk on the sandbags it would quickly wear them out.

At high tide people were forced to not only walk on the sandbags but under the remains of the houses. It gave one pause to be forced to walk under the foundation of a damaged house dangling 30 feet overhead. The metal pilings holding up one of the houses were already bending under the weight of the structure and potentially any of the houses could collapse at any moment.

I thought that if the houses are not removed before the summer the town would have to try to prohibit the public from using this side of the beach. The homeowners would have essentially privatized what is legally a public beach.

Even so, the sandbag seawall was not really working. During the high course tides ten-foot waves continued to crash halfway into the undersides of the buildings. It must be frightening to try to sleep when your house was shuddering from the impact of every wave.

If the houses were not removed they could end up being stranded on their pilings thirty feet out to sea. The first time I saw this phenomenon was on Dauphin Island in Alabama. My first thought was how clever of the homeowners. They had built their homes in the Gulf of Mexico so they could fish off their porch. It was only later that I realized the houses had originally been sitting on the sand and a hundred feet of beach had been washed out from under the houses during a single storm. The same thing could happen on Plum Island but the houses would be left sitting on stilts, not in the calm waters of the Gulf of Mexico, but in the stormy Atlantic.

It would be the final chapter in an unnecessary tragedy that started when water and sewer lines where buried beneath the beach in 2004. That construction encouraged homeowners to build permanent homes on a beach that is destined to erode 50 to 100 feet landward during the coming decade of sea level rise. It would not be a pretty sight.

Aftermath

The second house to fall

CHAPTER 10
COME HELL OR HIGH WATER
March 10, 2013

Kathy Connors couldn't sleep. Twenty-foot waves were pounding the undersides of her Plum Island home. She used to love her dream house, but lately she had been referring to it as Misery Island.

Kathy usually felt safe when Bob was at home. He seemed to know how to deal with any situation. He had designed this house to be able to survive a Category 3 Hurricane. It rested on hundred foot pilings sunk fifty feet into the beach. But Kathy wasn't so sure about Mother Nature. She seemed determined to wash away all the sand from beneath their Plum Island home.

The day before, Kathy had watched as their neighbor's house swayed, shivered and toppled into the surf. Last night the Bresnahan's house on the other side had groaned, then crumpled onto the beach. It had been like listening to a large animal gasp, collapse and die. Now a mass of water-soaked rugs, chairs and mattresses surged back and forth in the incoming tide and their neighbor Steve Bandoian's refrigerator was drifting toward Portugal.

Bob had led a constant stream of cops, politicians, and camera crews through the house for the past few months. Kathy had to watch as their muddy boots ground sand, snow and ice into her newly polished floors and just cleaned carpets.

Sleep deprived and a little nervous. Sam Joslin, Captain O'Reilly and Representative Mira giving the daily briefing from Bob Connor's shaky front deck.

And now their house was the nerve center for the immediate crisis. Every morning Senator Tarr would hold a press conference on the Connor's deck. Then the cameras would turn toward their neighbors' homes and the deathwatch would begin.

Bob was always at the senator's side, shaking hands, offering food, puffing on his cigar and leaning over the deck to give instructions to the excavator operator placing 5,000-pound concrete blocks beneath his home. The state considered such devices illegal because they increased erosion on downstream lots. But Senator Tarr had urged Bob to go ahead anyway. The senator would cover his back.

Bob was a man in control; in control of the message, in control of the political process, in control of the rules and regulations devised by humans to deal with the proposition of living beside the Atlantic Ocean.

He had already convinced Congressman Tierney to have Congress pay the Army Corps of Engineers $9 million dollars of the tax payer's money to fix the Merrimack River jetty. His main argument was that it would somehow protect homeowners from erosion half a mile away. He had also convinced his neighbors to spend thousands of dollars to scrape the beach and build a quarter mile long seawall of sandbags.

None of these engineering solutions had worked, nor would the 5,000-pound concrete blocks beneath his home, because the one thing that Bob was not in control of was Mother Nature. And right now Mother Nature was calling the shots in the guise of the fourth major blizzard to batter this coast since Hurricane Sandy.

Twenty-foot waves, a nine-foot high tide and a two-foot storm surge were battering the undersides of Bob and Kathy's house. The waves had already torn a gaping hole through their garage floor. The press couldn't help looking into the abyss of churning white water before climbing the stairs to Bob's deck that was shaking from the impact of every wave. It was like staring into a watery version of hell.

Bob still paced back and forth across his deck at the sun was setting. He looked like the captain of a ship, the captain of his own destiny. But the captain that Bob most resembled was Captain Ahab and it was Moby Dick getting ready to bash in the bottom of Bob's Plum Island home.

In the days following the storm it became clear what had actually happened. Virtually all the houses on the primary dune had
been damaged and would have to be torn down. Plum Island was
the most concentrated area of coastal erosion of anywhere on the
East Coast except New Jersey.

Bob's Annapolis Way neighborhood had lost forty homes, thirty
percent of its housing stock. The homeowners felt betrayed and
with good reason, they had been sold a bill of goods.

In one night nature had done to Plum Island what humans
should have been doing for several years, reducing the number
of houses on this fragile barrier beach. They had had their first
opportunity during the Seventies.

After scientists learned that barrier beaches had to be able to
move, environmental agencies started to devise regulations designed to protect homeowners from erosion, and barrier beaches
from overdevelopment. But the regulations contained loopholes
so wide that any developer with enough money, and political connections could easily circumvent the law. If that failed there were
always the courts.

In the early Seventies Plum Island had gone through a period of
intense erosion during several years when the highest tides had
fallen during the winter months. These tides had made the island
particularly vulnerable to erosion as they had in 2013.

The Army Corps of Engineers had been brought in to see if they
could solve the problem. As part of their pitch to get the job, the
Corps had warned of an earlier study that showed that the island

was in danger of breaking in two. Serious consideration was given to the idea of starting to turn over eroded properties to the immediately adjacent Parker River Federal Wildlife Refuge. It would have prevented the present situation.

But, the town fathers and local construction magnates, who were often, one and the same, decided that Plum Island was simply too valuable for tax revenues to just give away. The island would eventually provide the cash-strapped town of Newbury with 40% of its tax earnings. Plus the town wouldn't have to expend more money on things like schools because most the island's residents were wealthy and well beyond their child rearing years.

By 2004 the island had attained urban density and people were starting to get sick from drinking well water contaminated by her cheek by jowl cesspools. But, instead of taking steps to gradually reduce the population on the island, town, state and federal agencies had colluded to bury municipal water and sewer lines in the fragile barrier beach dunes. These were the same lines that had been damaged during Hurricane Sandy putting 750 households at risk.

Almost every environmental regulation had been bent or broken to put the lines in. The result? Now people who used to own simple summer cottages worth $3,000 to $4,000, started winterizing, modernizing and building new homes. Soon there was a row of million dollar mansions on top of the primary dunes where they enjoyed the most expensive waterfront views.

Formerly, when a homeowner lost his summer cottage he was able to walk away from his loss content that he had spent fifty or sixty wonderful years in a house worth under $20,000. But now people's entire family savings were wrapped up in their primary homes and their loss could be life altering. Many of the people who lost their homes would end up spending the rest of their lives in nursing homes. No wonder homeowners felt like they had been deceived when the government had provided them with the infrastructure to build their island homes.

Instead of using these critical junctures to gradually reduce number of houses on the island, the town fathers had created a situation where nature would do it for them. Now it would be interesting to see whether the town of Newbury could learn from its past mistakes and take steps to gradually reduce its footprint on this one small island. If it could, then perhaps we can also do the same for our entire planet. If not, nature will do it for us, because she always writes the last chapter.

CHAPTER 11
A CONVENIENT MYTH
March 25, 2013

If you look at the history of Plum Island you can see why her houses are washing away. Ten thousand years ago the ocean was 250 feet lower and this coast was almost five miles further east.

But the glaciers of the last Ice Age were melting fast and sediment from the White Mountains was rushing down what would become the Merrimack River to form a broad delta of Paleolithic sand. Waves and currents started reshaping this sand into a long thin barrier beach and pushibg it Westward. Plum Island had been born.

But the ocean was rising at the rate of about a foot every century. This gradual rise in sea level is enough to cause barrier beach islands like Plum Island to migrate slowly toward the mainland, through rollover.

You can see the difference between a developed and a natural beach at the Parker River Wildlife Refuge immediately adjacent to the houses on Plum Island. The dunes on the natural beach are almost twenty feet higher than the dunes where houses have prevented the dunes from growing and healing themselves.

Rollover is a one-way process that started to speed up about twenty years ago when the rate of sea level rise increased from about a foot every hundred years to a foot and a half every hundred years. This was because the volume of the ocean has increased as the temperature of their waters rose by about one degree Celsius. You can see the results of this change when you visit your favorite beach. The beach that you remember as a kid being a hundred feet wide now laps the dunes at high tide.

Geologists use a handy little rule of thumb called Bruun's Rule to calculate how far the beach will retreat as the seas rise. The rule states that every foot of sea level rise will cause beaches to retreat by a hundred to three hundred feet laterally. How fast this will happen depends on the number of major storms, which have become increasingly frequent due to global warming. In fact Plum Island lost up to 260 feet during the last 20 years but 40 feet during the four storms in February and March alone!

But none of these mainstream scientific explanations made any sense to Cheryl Comeau. I saw her at a Plum Island barbecue on March 25th. It was a bittersweet affair. Nobody knew if they would be able to move back into their condemned homes for the summer. Cheryl took particular pride in her blue-collar roots and wanted me to know that the island was not just made up of rich white guys used to getting their own way.

"It's funny, when I grew up here as a kid, Plum Island was referred to as Slum Island. We came from a family of carpenters. My father owned a maintenance shop with three employees. My mother and father are living there now. We had to move them there after the last storm."

"Their neighbors on Fordham Way were a retired school teacher and a janitor. In the old days poor people bought summer cottages on Plum Island because they were cheap."

But those days are certainly over. In 2008 a group of Plum Island residents formed the Plum Island Foundation in order to raise $60,000 a year to retain Marlowe and Company a Washington based firm whose expertise is in lobbying Congress and cutting through red tape on behalf of clients trying to deal with agencies like the Army Corps of Engineers, the EPA and the Federal Emergency Management Administration.

It is this lobbying group that prepared the talking points that most of the homeowners used when talking to the press. Like Bob Connors, Cheryl stuck closely to the talking points. She was adamant that global warming and sea level rise were nothing but a fraud foisted on the American people by a bunch of scientists and bureaucrats. To her it was all about jobs and money.

She reiterated the Marlowe Company's argument that the reason her family lost their home was because the Army Corps of Engineers had built a jetty almost a mile away.

But that was not all. The government agencies established under President Nixon to protect people from building on barrier beaches were to blame because now they wouldn't let her family use their own money to build a new artificial dune in front of their house. It would be similar to the artificial dune that the state said had increased erosion in front of Bob Connors' house.

The Marlowe and Company argument is the result of the way the Army Corps of Engineers is required to get its contracts. In the old days powerful Congressmen simply persuaded their colleagues to swap votes for their favorite pork barrel Army Corps of Engineers project. Now it was no fun. The Corps had to prepare

a cost benefit analysis to make sure that the cost of doing something like building a jetty would be outweighed by benefits to the
local community. But that was a hard sell for Newburyport that
was a relatively insignificant port that only served a fleet of small
pleasure boats.

There was simply not enough boat traffic to make the numbers
work so Marlowe and Company convinced the Corps to add in the
potential benefits of using sand dredged from the river to protect
Plum Island homes from erosion. It was a curious argument that
essentially said that jetties were the problem but that fixing them
was the solution. It could be argued that the simpler solution
would be to leave the jetties as is and dredge the river as needed
for navigational purposes.

But it didn't really matter. The cost benefit analysis allowed the
project to sail through Congress and gave the homeowners the
convenient myth that it was the Army Corps of Engineers not sea
level rise that was the cause of their problems.

The myth held sway for several years. Homeowners firmly
believed in it and were good at presenting it on television. They
convinced politicians like Senator Tar to repeat their point of view
and this had cowed government agencies into letting homeowners
do things like scraping the beach and putting in sandbag seawalls
that only increased the Plum Islanders problems.

But everything changed after the Plum Island Blizzard. The entire Massachusetts coast, all 1500 miles of it, had been eroded back 20 feet. Was all that erosion caused by the jetties on the Merrimack River?

CHAPTER 12
THE MEETING
March 26, 2013

Mark Richey has three passions; woodworking, mountain climbing and his new Plum Island home. His infectious smile and boyish charm underlie someone who approaches everything he does with thoroughness, enthusiasm and an appreciation for quality.

As a young man, Mark apprenticed himself to a master harpsichord builder and started making fine cabinetry in the basement of his apartment building in Malden, Massachusetts. At night he studied architecture at the Boston Architectural Center.

By 2013 he had parlayed his passion for woodworking into one of the largest woodworking and design companies in North America employing over 80 craftsmen. His longest serving employee was Mark's original mentor who had taught him how to build harpsichords back in 1979.

Today Mark Richey's workmanship can be found in schools libraries, corporations and private homes throughout the country. Everything is designed and built in his state of the art workshop in Newburyport, Massachusetts. His most recent additions to this 130,000-foot facility are a wind turbine to provide power and a biomass furnace to mold his bent wood furniture designs.

Mark's other great passion is mountain climbing, which he started doing in the Quincy Quarries at age 15. Since then he has summited some of the most difficult mountains in the world on over 40 expeditions. It was on an expedition to Peru that he met and married his wife Teresa who helped him co-found their wood working company. From the beginning she did everything in the shop from staining, to finishing to installing the final woodwork. Today she oversees the finances and administration of one of the most successful woman owned wood working companies in the country.

But the Richey's most recent passion was designing and building their Plum Island home. They poured all their expertise into the four-story house. You can see the sun rising out of the Atlantic from every room and watch it creep across exotic hardwood floors and sparkle off expensive imported stonework.

The only problem is, they had moved in only six days before the Plum Island Blizzard had torn away the primary dune in front of their home.

They had followed the state's regulations to a "T" building their house on steel beams driven a 40 feet into the sand. During the process of applying for permission to build their home nobody had ever mentioned to the Richeys that it was likely that their dune would wash away. Then, in the confusion following the storm the statements of their local representatives persuaded them that they would not be fined if they built an illegal seawall to protect their new house.

But the next week all the homeowners had received a letter from Ken Kimmel the Commissioner of the Massachusetts Department of Environmental Protection carefully explaining that armoring the beach would increase the amount of erosion in front of their homes and warned them that the walls would have to be removed at the owners expense by the end of the winter storm season.

On March 26th over 200 Plum Islanders attended a meeting to decide how to proceed. Toward the end of the meeting Steve Bandoian choked up as he recounted the loss of his Plum Island home and chastised Ken Kimmel and the DEP for letting it happen.

"Wake up people. It's time for the DEP to get the hell out of the way. They have an agenda and it doesn't include us. They want us gone."

"That island is permanent and it belongs there."

It was a perfect example of the 1950's mindset that believed that barrier beach islands are immovable features that have been in the same place for thousands of year. His comments drew loud applause and shouts of encouragement because it is still a popular misconception among homeowners and barrier beach developers.

But Steve had a point. The destruction of 39 homes had been an unnecessary tragedy. It never would have happened if people had been discouraged from building on the barrier beach in the first place.

After it was discovered that islands move in the Seventies, almost every coastal state promulgated regulations to prohibit building homes on barrier beaches. They were meant to protect both the beaches that needed to be able to move, and homeowners who stood to lose their life's savings if their houses washed away.

The regulations seemed like reasonable responses to sea level rise until they ran smack dab into the Constitution of the United States. After hearing a number of land use cases, The Supreme

Court ruled in Lucas vs. South Carolina in 1992, that if a state passed a regulation that reduced the value of someone's land it constituted a "taking" under the 5th Amendment and the state would have to compensate the homeowner for his loss. The ruling put the fear of death into cash strapped states. How could you enforce meaningful environmental regulations if you couldn't pass laws with any teeth?

So, instead of banning houses outright on barrier beaches states had to pass all kinds of half measures that suggested that homeowners should consider moving their homes off primary dunes or put them up on pilings to get them out immediate danger.

It could be argued that people would have been better off if they had been banned outright from building houses on Plum Island, instead of being put in jeopardy in only a few years - or in only 6 days, as had been the case with the Richey's.

CHAPTER 13
THE PROPOSAL
March 26, 2013

Marc Sarkady combed his long hair back behind his ears and adjusted his Navy Blue jacket. He had the stylish good looks of a hip businessman who felt just as comfortable in an academic seminar as a corporate boardroom.

He was the Washington based lawyer who had put together the Plum Island Foundation and hired Marlowe and Company to shepherd the Merrimack River jetties through the Army Corps of Engineers. He was the go-to guy when the chips were down and the chips were certainly down after the March storm.

He stole the show at the rancorous meeting in Newbury. After Steve Bandoian had finished telling the state officials to go to hell, Marc had thanked Senator Tarr for setting up the meeting even though he had to miss his family Passover to attend. Then he turned to address the head of the Department of Environmental Protection.

"In the spirit of Passover I would us to all remember Moses words to Pharaoh, "Let our people go. Let us do this thing."

Ken Kimmel smiled and the audience heaved a sigh of relief. Marc had helped deflate some of the ire of former speakers so the meeting could move on to get something done. It was the kind of menschy charm that had used so many times when he was con-sulting for some of the top Fortune 500 businesses. He had also helped negotiate the improved hotline between Washington and Moscow and had been a frequent mediator during environmental negotiations.

His note of goodwill had been matched by the head of the DEP who promised to consider the homeowners proposal to build an artificial sand dune.

The problem was, the proposal not very good. It was the essentially the same proposal that the homeowners had submitted before but now instead of calling it beach scraping they were calling it beach mining. It was a distinction without a difference. The sand was still going to be removed from the low tide beach and piled up into a loose conglomeration of unconsolidated sand that would wash away during the next storm as it had when they tried it back in September.

But the homeowners had fallen into the habit of only listening to what they wanted to hear, namely that if they spent another ten or twenty thousand dollars they could build something new to stop erosion in its tracks and save their homes. There were any number of firms who were only to happy to oblige with plans for dunes, beach scraping and sand bag seawalls.

What the homeowners really needed, however, was for someone to give them an honest evaluation of the situation -- namely that there were no feasible engineering solutions capable of stopping erosion in front of their homes.

It was inevitable that more of their houses would have to be moved, but there were ways to slow down the rate of erosion and possibly give homeowners a few more years to enjoy their beach-front homes. But to do it, you would have to work with the forces of nature not against them. Finally I decided to throw in my two cents on the matter.

Working with Nature.

Pondering the Groins

CHAPTER 14
WORKING WITH NATURE
April 2, 2013

My time arrived in early April. The local paper had run an aerial photo taken by the Plum Island Taxpayer's Association to support the beach mining proposal. Its caption repeated the convenient myth that sand flows north to south on Plum Island. In fact it showed exactly the reverse.

The dominant flow of sand on Plum Island was from south to north, from the undeveloped beach in front of the Parker River Refuge in the center of the island toward the Merrimack River. You could see where the longshore currents had deposited scalloped shaped crescents of sand on the south side of a series of old groins and the jetties were shooting all that valuable sand into deep water where it would be lost to the system.

But the most important thing that the photo showed was how quickly the natural beach was healing itself. The winter's storms had eroded hundreds of thousands of cubic yards of sand out of the center of the island, so that the undeveloped beach now was more than a hundred feet wide and its dunes were 10 to 20 feet higher than the dunes on the developed beach. There was almost no beach in front of the developed beach because of the seawalls, groins and beach scraping projects that had increased the amount of erosion in front of the threatened homes.

But I felt the photo also pointed toward an inexpensive solution, so I wrote an OPED piece in the Newburyport Current. The article opened by saying that you could not stop erosion but that there was a way to work with nature to slow it down.

It explained that the old groins were blocking the sand released by the winter storms from flowing north to build up a natural beach in front of the threatened homes. If these groins were removed or shortened that sand would be able to move freely north. Waves would then tamp down the sand to form a firm consolidated natural beach in front of the vulnerable homes.

The reason that the September beach scraping failed is that it had just pushed up a big pile of loose and unconsolidated sand that had washed away during hurricane Sandy. A natural firm beach would be far more resilient.

Beach "mining" had appeared to work after the 1978 blizzard for the same reason. The blizzard released so much natural sand into the system that it had protected the artificial dune, and the beach went into an apparent erosional lull. This often happens after major storms because they sweep away all the most vulnerable homes and add large amounts of sand that can protect the remaining homes for a few more years.

The other reason that the 1978 artificial sand dune appeared to work was that sea levels were lower then. The Atlantic Ocean was a good 4 inches lower in 1978. Four inches might not seem like a lot, but according to Bruun's Rule, that translates into 3.3 to 10 feet of lateral erosion. The Army Corps of Engineers had calculated that Plum Island was already eroding laterally at the rate of about 13 feet of sand a year, and almost 40 feet of sand had washed away from beneath people's homes during just the last four months.

I expected people to balk at the idea of removing old anti-ero-
sional devices. We have become so enamored with trying to
armor the coast, that the idea of removing such things as groins
might seem counterintuitive. But it is a little like removing a dam
to improve the natural flow of a river.

The jetties keeping the Merrimack River open were the result of
another counterintuitive idea. In 1876 the Mississippi River was
so silted up that ocean going vessels were not able to enter the
mouth of the river. Dredging had become ineffective and prohibitively expensive. But a Mississippi salvager had a radical idea.

James Eads had spent most of his early years in a heavy diving
helmets walking along the bottom of the Mississippi looking for
sunken cargo. It was a lucrative business -- more cargo resides
on the bottom of the Mississippi River than on its surface.

Eads knew how effective currents could be at scouring deep
holes out of the bottom of the treacherous river. He felt that if
you could constrict the mouth of the river between two jetties the
resultant currents would scour out the mouth of the river. He was
so sure of his idea that he agreed to form a private company and
fund the project himself.

He was bitterly opposed by Major Howell of the Army Corps
of Engineers, who was determined to maintain the comfortable
monopoly the Army Corps of Engineers had enjoyed since its
incorporation under George Washington. Who did this self-taught
upstart think he was telling them how to dredge their river?

The controversy came to a head on May 12, 1876. The Corps
leaked information to the press that Howells measurements
showed that the Mississippi was only 12 feet deep and that Ead's

jetties had failed. The news caused stocks in Ead's company to tumble. He knew his only chance for redemption lay in an ocean-going steamship that lay just offshore. It was the *Hudson*, a three hundred foot vessel that drew fourteen feet seven inches of water. She was under the command of Captain E.V. Gagner, Eads' old friend from their early days in St. Louis.

Gagner welcomed Eads aboard; along with several journalists that Eads had invited to chronicle his gamble. They knew the stakes were as high as on any riverboat poker table back in New Orleans.

Gagner knew the danger of the situation as well. The tide was falling fast and his local pilot had recommended that he not attempt to cross the bar. But Gagner did not hesitate.
"Head for the jetties."

On shore three hundred men ceased their labors to watch. They too knew the stakes, as the ship started to build up a head of steam.

"Shall we run in slow?"

"No sir let her go in at full speed."

Gagner knew the increased speed would lift the *Hudson*' s bow a few inches above the surface of the water and push her stern a few inches below it. If Eads were correct they would just skim over the mud, but if Major Howell were correct the *Hudson* would tear out her hull and sink to the bottom.

The *Hudson* gained speed and a huge white wake billowed out ahead of her bows then separated into a long "V" that sloshed the edges of the willow-sided jetties. One of the journalists wrote, "As long as she carried that white bone in her great wave that her proud bows pushed ahead of, sped forward – we knew that she had found more than Howell's 12 feet. "

Then she was through. Captain Gagner blew a powerful blast on the *Hudson*'s steam whistle and three hundred men erupted into cheers that reverberated up and down Mississippi Delta as the great ship made her way majestically north.

I closed my article by asking people to look at the aerial photo once again, you could see that during the coming summer the natural beach was going to continue to grow higher and wider while the developed beach was going to continue to stay thin and vulnerable. I suggested that like Eads, people start thinking about working with the forces of nature not against them. Unlike the flamboyant articles about Ead's triumph in the Picayune Times, my article in the Newburyport Current landed like a lead balloon!

Santa Catalina

CHAPTER 15
NOBODY CARES WHAT ACTORS THINK!
April 5, 2013

On April 5th I flew to the West Coast to get some much needed rest on Catalina Island, to give a talk at the Aquarium of the Pacific and to see how Californians deal with coastal erosion -- pretty much in that order of personal preference.

While Santa Catalina is hardly an "Island in the Storm", I knew from the song it was 26 miles at sea. More boats visit the island than any other location on the West Coast. I caught the early morning ferry from Long Beach. We slipped quietly past the Queen Mary tied up rather sadly at dock and steamed past scores of container vessels waiting to get into one of the busiest ports in the country. As we left the harbor we passed three islands festooned with oil derricks built to look like art deco palm trees, only in California!

Then we rode through empty waters until the mountainous physiognomy of Catalina loomed out of California's ever-present morning fog. Through the mist we could see tiny white cottages nestled into steep ravines. I felt like I could have been approaching a cozy lakeside village in southern Switzerland.

But this was the playground for folks like John Wayne, Marilyn Monroe, General Patton, and of course the gorgeous Natalie Wood who died under still suspicious circumstances while swimming off her husband's yacht in Catalina Harbor.

The art deco façade of the Catalina Casino rose on the far side of the harbor. It used to house the largest circular dance floor in the country and was a favorite gig for Big Band musicians who took the ferry to the island every week to play in concerts broadcast throughout the country.

Their curiously heavy instrument cases often dripped drops of amber fluid and their all night drinking parties were the stuff of legend. Baseball players from the Chicago Cubs often wandered into the parties from their nearby spring training camp. The musicians and baseball players were there thanks to the largess of the chewing gum magnate William Wrigley. Every island has to have a big man, and on Catalina it was William Wrigley.

Hollywood shot scores of films and television shows on Catalina and Zane Gray started the big game fishing industry on the island then released a herd of bison that still roam through the rugged interior today.

I watched dolphins, seals, tiger sharks, and large orange Garibaldis gamboling in the shallows within twenty feet of the shore. It was a busman's holiday after a long cold winter.

But I had to eat a little crow at the Aquarium of the Pacific. The last time I spoke there I gave a long lecture about all the wonderful things we had done in Chatham Massachusetts. I explained that by using a camera mounted on the mainland I had been able to tell homeowners they had between 8 and 10 days, then 5 and 6 days, and then 2 and 3 days before their houses were swept out to sea.

But eventually we fine-tuned the system so well that we were able to help homeowners move their fishing camps out of harm's way. In the end the homeowners spent over $100,000 to move the last five remaining camps into a new village a tenth of a mile up the beach. But then an unexpectedly late June storm washed the entire village away.

When I finished my talk some guy in the back of the audience piped up, "Don't you guys have any laws back there in Massa-chusetts?" I mumbled some kind of answer but the question had taken me by surprise. It was the "Aha" moment I needed. Sudden-ly I realized I had become so caught up in moving the houses, that I had lost sight of the ultimate futility of the endeavor.

This time I spoke about Plum Island but explained rhetorically, "Actually we do have some pretty good laws in Massachusetts. It is just that we have been encouraged not to obey them."

But Plum Island doesn't hold a candle to the sense of enti-tlement that people have in LA. In nearby Malibu, charismatic entertainers like Goldie Hawn, Steven Spielberg, Dustin Hoffman why even Robert Redford are lined up against the poor little Los Angeles Department of Beaches. The actors are pushing to get permission to use offshore sand to build an artificial $20 million dollar sand dune to protect their Broad Beach homes. However, the LA Department of Beaches owns the sand and wants to save it to use on public beaches threatened by sea level rise.

Broad Beach's homeowners have had a long-standing history of enmity against the public. For years, they hired armed security guards to harass sunbathers, and in 2005, 108 of the homeown-ers stole tons of sand off a neighboring public beach to build another sand dune in front of their homes.

Although it was illegal not much had happened except that the dune had washed away. Then, in 2010 the state gave homeowners permission to build a $4 million dollar sharp rock seawall that effectively prevented surfers and sunbathers from using the public beach.

I had the distinct feeling that the rich and famous were going to win again. It seemed to be a pattern repeating itself on both the left and right sides of our country.

Marilyn Monroe on Catalina Island

CHAPTER 16
A TURNING POINT?
Plum Island April 9, 2013

Back in March it looked like someone had just dropped a bomb on Plum Island. Three houses were washing back and forth in the surf, three were being hastily demolished and thirty more had been declared uninhabitable.

All you could see were large, gangly looking, yellow excavators tearing great chunks of wood and plaster out of the sides of houses then spinning around to spit them into the maws of large idling trucks. They looked like a herd of meat eating dinosaurs tearing into the flesh of a dying Triceratops.

All you could hear was the roar of trucks as they rumbled through the narrow streets and the thuds of 5,000 pound concrete blocks, as they were dumped onto the beach where more excavators rearranged them into retaining walls in front of individual homes. Other trucks and excavators were dumping more rocks on the beach. By the end of the month a massive wall of concrete blocks, and sharp misshapen rocks had transformed Plum Island. It looked like the riprap and wreckage left on Omaha Beach the day after the Normandy Invasion.

But by mid-April it looked as if nothing had happened. The illegal seawall had been carefully buried under tons of imported sand. The beach was quiet and clean, calmly awaiting the arrival of piping plovers, those controversial little endangered shorebird that had flown all the way up from the coast of South America to lay their eggs on Plum Island.

Despite its new appearance, everything had just changed on the island. Now, instead of facing a solid wall of imposing homes lined up on the primary dune, there were 7 gaps where the former houses had been. Townspeople could now walk along Annapolis Way, gaze out over the Atlantic Ocean and have access to the middle of one of the best beaches in New England. It was not lost on some of the homeowners in the secondary dunes that the value of their land had also just increased because they now enjoyed ocean views.

A turning point?

But these changes were not destined to last. Massachusetts's officials had given homeowners permission to build the artificial sand dune and the Newbury Conservation commission had given three homeowners permission to elevate and rebuild their homes on exactly the same footprint as before. It had been a strange meeting. None of the commissioners seemed to be conservationists and nobody mentioned that according to the Army Corps of Engineers the houses would wash away again in the next two to five years. The only discussions involved how to hook up the house to utilities and how many pilings to drive. All the votes were unanimous.

It looked like Newbury was intent on making all the same mistakes it had made before, to be locked in this never ending cycle of erosion, destruction, rebuilding and more destruction, to continue being the poster child for everything a community shouldn't do to combat sea level rise.

But there was also a glimmer of hope. One wise and brave homeowner had embarked on a different route. He had taken the Federal government up on its offer to purchase his property in exchange for giving his lot to the town to be used as a seaside park along with his adjacent parking lot.

The only kicker was that the Feds would only pay 75% of the fair market value of the preexisting property; the town would have to come up with the remaining 25%.

This put me on the horns of a dilemma. Usually I like to write about such topics as an outside observer. But I had started the Coastlines Program, a non-profit organization established to help communities cope with the effects of sea level rise. We had helped start "The Friends of Pleasant Bay" that had ended up buying several plots of endangered land that had become open space areas where the public could walk and have access to the water.

A group of concerned citizens had also just put together an informal new organization called Sea Level Rise, Newburyport Plus. They were holding their second meeting and someone from New Hampshire was going to speak about their coastal adaptation plans. This seemed like it was bringing coals to Newcastle. New Hampshire has the smallest coast in the nation; it only has eighteen miles of sand, gravel and marshes.   Why even the four towns affected by Plum Island had a much longer coast than that! But it was a start.

I also approached Newbury's town manager with the idea of setting up a buyout fund. I argued that if each of the thousands of people who cherished Plum Island paid $35 to join "The Friends of Plum Island," Newbury would have the $222, 800 it needed to pay for its share of the lot slated for buyout. The fund could also be funded by charging homeowners a small fee or assessing them for a half a percent of the cost of rebuilding their home.

Their money would be reimbursed to them many times over if they signed up for the buyout program at a later date. In the end the owner of the lot would get the full market value of his preexisting home, the town would get a park and adjacent parking lot in perpetuity, not a bad deal in my book.

I waited with baited breath to see if either approach would work or would simply land with the same resounding thud as had those 5,000 pound concrete blocks now hiding illegally underneath several thousand tons of imported sand!

Preparing to move Milton Tzitzenikos' house across Annapolis Way.

CHAPTER 17
MILTON TZITZENIKOS
April 12, 2013

Milton Tzitzenikos is one of the old timers on Plum Island. The 87 year old veteran first started coming to Island in the 1940's when you could still buy one of the shacks for three or four thousand dollars.

"The one we bought was built kind of funny. Most of the shacks built back then were built from pieces of driftwood. So I went down to the Five Cent Savings Bank and borrowed $10,000 so we could start fixing 'er up."

"I did most of the work himself, just a little of this, a little of that. One of the first things we had to do was build a road, just a little path really, so we could get into the house."

"It was pretty Tobacco Road back then but we had a wonderful time. It was just the best place in the world to catch fish. We would go down to the Ipswich end of the island to dig for clams. But we also caught a lot of bloodworms so we would save these and keep them for bait.'

"We would catch stripers and sand dab right in front of the house. And when the water cooled down a bit, you could catch cod and silver hake. Phyllis would fry them up in our wood-burning stove. The whole house would smell of fish sautéing briskly in olive oil. It makes me hungry right now. Those were wonderful days."

In 1990 Milton borrowed another $125,00 to rebuild. About four years ago the ocean was still several hundred feet away and the house was assessed at $1,200,000. But it dropped down to

$800,000 as the ocean got closer. Milton and all of his neighbors had to be evacuated from their houses after a March storm in 2010 made their houses uninhabitable.

Sam Joslin let the neighbors rebuild their homes but the ocean was so close their assessments dropped again. That was when Milton's neighbor John Drinkwater gave up the battle and lowered the price on his house from $800,000 to $300,000. It was scooped up instantly by Bob Connor's cousin Dave Williamson who tore down John's house and built a much larger one on pilings only twenty feet back from the ocean.

These were the same houses that would be in trouble only three short years later. But while his neighbors' houses were tumbling into the ocean, during the 2013 blizzard, Milton had the foresight to quietly remove his house from its foundation and put it up on blocks in his driveway.

"We raised four children and five grandchildren in that house. Two of my daughters are attorneys. Now they are working with the DEP to see if we can move the house to our old parking lot on the other side of Annapolis Way.

"But I don't have insurance. After the last storm they wanted $7,000. Now they want $100,000 to move the house and raise it up on pilings. Then you still have to pay for water and electricity hookups. I'm a barber for God's sake I don't got no money."

It would be a lot of money to lose. It would also a lot of money for the town to lose. Most of the owners paid $13,000 to $14,000 in taxes. Nine tenths of that was for the waterfront property and only one tenth was for the building.

But unlike some of his younger neighbors this unassuming veteran who had stormed LeHavre when he was only eighteen years old did not blame the DEP for his problems. "I don't know, New Jersey got hit too."

"We enjoyed it so much out there. We hope to stay back up on pilings on the other side of Annapolis Way. But what happens, happens." Phyllis agreed, "We had forty-six years out there, forty-six years of wonderful memories."

But there was another option. One of Milton's neighbors was looking into a new experimental FEMA program specifically designed to help communities like Plum Island solve its recurrent erosion problems.

Under this program, the federal government paid a homeowner 75% of the fair market value of his home, and the town would pay the remaining 25%. The homeowner would be free to retire to

Florida where there were fewer financial headaches but the fish wouldn't taste nearly as good as those cooked in their own Plum Island home.

Under the plan, the town would be deeded the rights to an seaside park where townspeople could gaze out over the ocean and have access to one of the best beaches in New England. It was not lost on the homeowners in the secondary dune that the value of their properties would also be increased because they could now see the ocean instead of looking at a solid wall of imposing homes lining the top of the shifting primary dune.

"Let's recognize that there are some places that
Mother Nature owns. She may only come to visit
every two, or three or every four years. But when
she comes to visit, she reclaims the site. I want to be
there for people and communities who want to say,
I'm going to give this parcel back to Mother Nature."

-Governor Cuomo *February 26, 2013*

CHAPTER 18
THE RUBBER STAMP
April 16, 2013

On April 16th, I sat in on the Newbury Conservation Commission's regular monthly meeting. The purpose of the meeting was to decide whether three of the homeowners who lost their homes during the March storm could rebuild.

It was a strange meeting. Every town in Massachusetts is required to have a conservation commission established to make sure that homeowners and builders adhere to the state's Wetlands Protection Act. One of the regulations of the act states that people cant built hard structures like seawalls on barrier beaches because they interfere with the natural flow of sand up and down the beach.

This was a bit embarrassing, because all the applicants who were appearing before the commission had broken the law by putting rock walls in front of their former homes, and now they wanted to rebuild those homes on exactly the same footprint as before.

I had appeared before conservation commissions in several other towns. Normally they are made up of rather stern people in the environmental field and chaired by an especially stern senior member. The commissioners question the applicants closely, determine if there will be any environmental impacts from the proposed work, vote on the project then pass their decision on to the town conservation agent who is responsible for seeing that all the commission's recommendations are followed.

But this commission was different. It was chaired by the Conservation agent himself, and the majority of the members were in the construction business. Some of them had even built houses on Plum Island and one had built the artificial sand dune that the state had declared illegal in 1999.

When the three projects came up before the commission, there was no discussion about the environmental impact of building permanent structures on moving sand dunes, no data about what the beach was going to do, no debate about the wisdom of rebuilding on exactly the same footprints as before and no warning that the applicants would probably be back before the same commission after their second new home had also just tumbled into the ocean.

I could understand the motivations of the homeowners. They were driven by a deep-seated, almost biologically based sense of territoriality. This was their home, they owned the land, they had lived on the beach for twenty odd years, and no pointy-headed bureaucrat was going to tell them what to do with their land.

The fact that they might end up paying thousands of dollars in legal and engineering fees almost every year for the rest of their lives didn't seem to matter. They were determined to prove that they were right and the state DEP was wrong. I knew how they felt. I had felt the same way when my family's Cape Cod house had been on the line twenty years before.

It was more difficult to understand the motivations of the commission members. They were supposed to uphold the law and help owners make decisions based on mainstream science. But none of that happened during the meeting. The only questions revolved around how many pilings needed to be driven under each house, how to hook into water and electricity outlets and where to build egresses so the owners would be able to get out of their houses during upcoming storms. The conservation agent closed each case by saying, "We want you to be able to rebuild your house as quickly as possible and stay in it for as long as possible." He never mentioned that that might only be two to four years.

I had seen conservation commissions in other towns give homeowners permission to rebuild their barrier beach homes, but they had stipulated that this would be their last chance. The homeowners had to forfeit their eligibility for future tax supported flood insurance. It seemed to be a rational way to deal with sea level rise. Most people accepted the stipulations and took the deal even if they disagreed with its logic.

But these sorts of approaches were also not mentioned in this meeting. Each project was rubber stamped after a brief discussion and a unanimous vote. It was clear that Plum Island was going to be New England's poster child for sea level rise for years to come.

But there was a glimmer of hope. Three of the five positions on the commission were due to be refilled by the end of 2013.

Newbury is a small town and it might be difficult to find qualified people willing to volunteer to meet once a month but it did seem possible that the town could find commissioners who possessed more of an environmental ethic and had fewer conflicts of interest. However any new commissioner would have to be voted in by the Board of Selectmen, and that was its own kettle of fish.

The chairman of the board of selectmen had an anti-government bias and a grudge against the state's Department of Environmental Protection. That bias seemed to permeate most of the town's boards and committees. It was going to be a sticky wicket!

Bennett Hill

CHAPTER 19
"A WIN-WIN SITUATION"
May 5, 2013

The first thing you notice when you enter Staten Island is how selective Hurricane Sandy was when she devastated our coasts.

Six months after the storm, Oakwood Heights looks like nothing ever happened. Just a bunch of middle class homes clustered around the Oakwood Heights Railway station, but when you step across Hylan Avenue you enter a different world, a ghost town of its former self.

Oakwood Beach used to be a thriving working class community. It was the kind of neighborhood where everyone looked after their neighbors' homes and children played in the streets.

But now everyone was gone. Most of the houses were missing, only their empty foundations remained. A lone tire swing hanging from an old oak tree was the only reminder that children once played in this neighborhood of idyllic little bungalows.

Now Oakwood Beach would be remembered mostly for the three residents who died in their homes during Hurricane Sandy. Two of them had been Neil Filipowicz's brother and nephew. They both drowned in the twenty-foot waves and eight-foot storm surge that had flooded into their single family home.

Oakwood Beach had always been a world apart, a low-lying area of marshes and scrub oak beside the raging Atlantic. Its tallest feature was a mountain of household trash in the center of what had once been the largest manmade object on the face of the globe, and the nearby Fresh Kills Landfill.

Every day barges would dump 650 more tons of trash from Manhattan and New Jersey onto the artificial landform. Every day the mountain would grow a little taller. By 2001 it was 25 meters taller than the Statue of liberty and well on it's way to becoming the highest point on the East Coast.

On March 22, 2001 the landfill was closed under pressure from neighbors who feared its packs of feral dogs and hated its reputation as a dumping ground for crooks who got whacked by the mafia. But it was reopened only a few months later after 9/11. Fresh Kills was the only landfill on the East Coast close enough and large enough to accommodate all the rubble and bits and pieces of human remains from the World Trade Center.

But by 2012 most of the former landfill had been reclaimed into the marshes, swamps and oak forests of the Gateway National Park, New York City's largest recreational area, Fresh Kills Park, weighing in at three times larger than New York's Central Park.

Joe Tirone introduced the idea of a buyout to his neighbors a few days after Hurricane Sandy. About 200 dazed people were milling around the St Charles School auditorium. He polled his neighbors, and everyone in the room raised their hands. It was surprising but understandable.

They had suffered a decisive defeat. Almost everyone in the room had lost their homes. They had also been through this many times before. Their neighborhood had a long history of being devastated by the ocean storms and scrub oak forest fires.

In 1992 a Northeaster had flooded most of these same homes, and afterwards the Oakwood Beach neighborhood had banded together to try to get permission to build a berm to protect their community.

It had taken eight years but the group finally received permission to build the berm. But like all the other solutions it had not worked. Nobody harbored any false illusions that any kind of hard engineering solution would save their neighborhood this time either. Joe Monte said it best, "Mother Nature has taken my home back. It should not have been there from the beginning."

But all their organizing they had done after the 1992 storm paid off after Hurricane Sandy. They had stayed together as a group and were first in line and organized when FEMA came to town to explain its experimental buyout programs.

Joe formed the Oakwood Beach Buyout Committee that had eventually also caught the eye of Governor Cuomo who wanted a testing ground for his state plan to return parts of the seashore to nature to create storm buffers.

Now 185 former Oakwood Beach homeowners were pining their hopes on the pilot program. Joseph Monte was pleased with the option, "My home is ruined and surrounded by water. You can't even breathe in it, let alone enter it safely." Neil Filipowicz agreed. "This is exactly what should be done." His brother's house had been flooded several times before.

But perhaps Joseph Tirone said it best, "This is a win-win situation. People will be getting 100% of the preexisting value of their homes they could never get that on the open market. Even if you brought your property back to pre-storm conditions it would still be at a 50% discount. Nobody wants to live here and getting insurance would be prohibitively expensive."

Some of the residents also planned to apply for an additional 5% incentive for remaining together as a group and moving to a safer part of the borough. "Of course I want to stay on Staten Island," said Joe Monte from the stairs of his water soaked bungalow. "I love it here. I'm just done with the water."

CHAPTER 20
"THIS USED TO BE A HOUSE?"
Prince Harry May 14, 2013

Governor Christie chortled with delight when he first heard that Prince Harry would visit the Jersey Shore. The overweight Republican was a master at projecting a public persona. It was he who had lambasted President Obama all during the recent campaign election, then clasped the skinny young Democratic president in a made-for-TV bear hug after Hurricane Sandy. It was he who made fun of his own weight, then quietly had gastric bypass surgery just before running for reelection. Now it was he who had captured everyone's favorite royal, the dashing young prince with the bad boy reputation. Harry would be better at drawing attention to New Jersey's rebirth than half a dozen regular celebrities.

But Harry's handlers hadn't done their homework. They wanted to rehabilitate Harry's tarnished reputation after his last visit to the United States when his royal highness was caught cavorting naked in Las Vegas with a bevy of equally unclothed showgirls.

Evidently they had been playing a game of billiards whose main point seemed to be to remove an article of clothing and have a drink every time you missed a shot. Harry's game was off that night, as were his shorts, coat, pants and royal underwear. Much like his namesake, Prince Hal of the 14th Century, Harry liked to party. The hope prevailed in Buckingham Palace that he would eventually become a sober Windsor instead of a feckless Spencer.

If Harry's handlers hadn't watched the latest installment of Jersey Shore, Governor Christie certainly had. He knew there was no better celebrity to champion the cause of New Jersey than England's bad boy prince.

The last time a member of royal had visited the Jersey Shore it was for a more somber occasion. The world was teetering on the brink of war, and King George, the Stutterer, and one of the innumerable Queen Elizabeths, had stopped at Red Bank station on their way to visit President Roosevelt at his home in Hyde Park.

The purpose of that trip was to try to persuade the United States to go to war against Germany. The purpose of this trip was to celebrate the rebirth of New Jersey while incidentally rehabilitating Harry's reputation for louche and lascivious behavior.

The handlers had certainly tried. The trip was fully booked with charity events and wholesome athletic pursuits. But, this being Prince Harry, and this being the Jersey Shore of Snooki, the Situation, and lots of hot tubs; people wanted to know whether Harry had any extracurricular intentions.

On a talk show before the event, a caller asked Governor Christie if there were any plans to make sure Harry behaved himself. "The last time he visited the US he was caught on camera naked. This is not the kind of image we need for the Jersey Shore."

It might not have been the kind of image the Shore needed, but Christie knew that just the mere hint that something unscripted might happen was sure to garner widespread interest if not titillation.

"Everything will be fine," soothed Governor Christie. "I'm going to be spending the entire day with Prince Harry, so believe me nobody is going to get naked, OK? I can assure the people of New Jersey that Prince Harry and I will keep all of our clothes on. And I'm certainly sure they are relieved at that!"

Harry's British handlers played their part with characteristic understatement. Their Consulate to New York said she didn't have any knowledge that Prince Harry had any unofficial plans, "It is a very busy schedule."

There it was, handlers in both the U.S. and Great Britain doing their damnedest to keep their frisky young prince under control. You couldn't buy any better publicity than that!

The day went off without a hitch. Governor Christie acted like one of the teenage girls waiting for Harry to arrive. He twitted that the prince's helicopter was in sight, "It is still the best way to travel through this damaged area."

Unfortunately Harry couldn't order a bucket of Curley's Fries.
"There is still no power," confided an employee of the not yet fully functional Casino Pier.

True to his word, Governor Christie dressed in a striking lime green shirt and shades and stayed close to Harry during the entire day. They looked like a cross between The Odd couple and Men in Black.

On Montoloking, the wealthy barrier island where all of the 521 wealthy homes had been swept away or badly damaged the odd couple paused in front of a barren spot, "This used to be a House?" asked Harry incredulously.

In Seaside Heights they gazed at the iconic remains of the Jet Star Roller Coaster jutting out of the Atlantic Ocean. Sandy had swept it off the Casino Pier during the height of the storm.

A barge and large crane floated just offshore. As soon as the royal entourage passed the crane would start removing the twisted metal of the doomed roller coaster so daredevils wouldn't try to surf through its superstructure in future storms.

Harry looked a little bored but played along, shaking hands with first responders and throwing whiffle balls through holes in a board to win angry birds for his many young admirers.

The message was clear. The Jersey Shore was alive and well and ready for business. By the end of the day the press seemed resigned to the fact that they were not going to witness any untoward behavior. One passerby groused that he would have at least liked to have had a drink with the old Harry. The New Harry undoubtedly agreed.

But as far as Bill Akers was concerned the day had been a complete success. The mayor of Seaside Heights explained he had spent the last six months being constantly asked whether his town would be ready for the summer. "I would always reply, 'Oh no problem.' The truth of the matter was. I had no idea."

Harry ended the tour by saying what he was supposed to say, "New Jersey really shows a fantastic American spirit. Everyone getting together and making things right,"

But the truth of this matter was that nobody would have any idea if they had made things right until after they had gone through the upcoming hurricane season. It was easy and natural to say that everything had been rebuilt and would be fine after a major storm. But it was also still possible to fly down to Miami and see destroyed houses twenty years after Hurricane Andrew and to travel down to New Orleans and see that 30 % of her population had never returned after Katrina.

In fact many of the houses in New Orleans should never have been rebuilt in their former locations. Had New Jersey rebuilt its famed piers boardwalks and casinos in the wrong places as well?

CHAPTER 21
ROCKS FOR JOCKS
Coastal Geology 101 May 20, 2013

By mid-May another piece of evidence emerged off Plum Island. This time it was in the form of two sets of sandbars; one to the south toward Ipswich, and one to the north toward the Merrimack River. Both were to be expected.

The winter storms had eroded sand off the center of the island in the Parker River Refuge and created longshore currents, which flowed both north and south.

The offshore sand had not been immediately apparent because it was in well-dispersed underwater sandbars. As spring arrived however, longer period waves with less energy started to bunch up the sand up into offshore sandbars that could be seen at low tide.

The longer period waves were also pushing these sandbars shoreward. By May several of these transverse sandbars had attached to the beach by their south ends. They were now called oblique sandbars because they approach the beach at an oblique angle.

You can see similar offshore sandbars attaching to the beach at an oblique angle on almost any East Coast Beach. They indicate that sand is eroded off beaches by high energy, short period waves during winter storms, then is transported back to the beach by low energy longer period waves during calm summer weather. But the sandbars only appear to be migrating because one end attaches first.

Notice I haven't said anything about a current that is supposed to flow from the Merrimack River south. I don't doubt that such a current exists but it is offshore current and is of far less importance to the primary dynamics of sand flow on Plum Island.

The bottom line of this short discourse is that repairing the Merrimack River jetty will improve navigation in the river a lot. But it will do very little to protect the houses almost two miles away on Annapolis and Fordham Way. That had been the convenient fiction devised by the Army Corps to convince Congress to put up the money to dredge the Merrimack River.

But now people were gambling that their houses would be protected by this convenient fiction. It was not a safe bet in my humble opinion.

Harry Trout's old lot had been on the left side of Fordham Way, his new house is on the right.

CHAPTER 22
HARRY TROUT
Plum Island, May 22, 2013

Harry Trout glanced at his watch then looked out the window of his Plum Island home. The state inspector was due to arrive in ten minutes. Two months ago this street had been jammed with National Guard trucks and police cruisers.

He walked slowly across the street to the lot where his ocean-front home once stood. Now it was empty. Police tape cordoned off the lot. Only a small slab of painted concrete remained. The town had made him demolish his home after last March's storm, now he was applying for permission to rebuild.

He knew it was going to be a long drawn out process. The conservation commission had gone well, perhaps too well. After the meeting the state had written a letter informing him they were assuming jurisdiction over his application.

It was frustrating being singled out for review. Maybe it was his fault. He had been the first homeowner to submit his proposal. But it would have saved a step if the town hadn't rubber stamped his proposal quite so blatantly.

Now Harry wasn't sure how the state would react. He had been one of the people who had built the beginnings of an extra- curricular seawall. The recent high tides had already started to wash away the sand that the homeowners had brought in to cover the seawalls. Now the seawalls would become even more apparent as summer approached and people started to use the public beach. He knew the state had every right to make him remove the structure so he would be in compliance with the Wetlands Protection Act. He would just have to see if they were going to be hard on him, or easy on him.

Harry looked at his watch again. Now it was two minutes until 10 am. Finally a police cruiser pulled up followed by several town and state officials, two members of the conservation commission and two journalists.

But it turned out the seawall was not the state analyst's main concern. Michael Abell was worried that Harry's house was on almost the lowest coastal lot on Plum Island. During the March storm, waves had demolished the solid bulkhead of rock filled railroad ties in front of Harry's home, then flowed across the street and under the second and third tier of houses on the other side of Fordham Way.

If Plum Island were going to break in two this was probably where it would happen. If so, waves would break the mains below Fordham Way, leaving the southern end of the island without water and the neighborhood flooded with raw sewage. It would not be as bad as if the island broke at the center groin, which would leave 750 homes without sewer or water lines, but it would cause considerable inconvenience.

So now Harry had two options. He and his neighbors could either continue to apply for permission to rebuild and elevate their homes or they could look into the Federal buyout program. If they decided to rebuild they would have to elevate their homes on pilings at least two feet above the velocity zone. But when NOAA's new flood zone maps came out in the summer, it would cost $9,500 at year to insure a $250,000 home below the V-zone, $1,410 a year to insure it at base flood elevation and only $427 a year if you built it 3 feet above the velocity zone.

That meant you could save more than $95,000 over ten years on insurance, but it would cost between $30,000 and $40,000 to elevate your house that high. Plus you wouldn't be able to get a mortgage from the Newburyport's Institution for Savings. The local bank had decided that financing a Plum Island home was no longer a wise investment.

The National Flood insurance program didn't want to keep paying people to rebuild their houses on erosional hotspots either. So they had their two grant programs to help people living on places like Plum Island. The coastal hazards mitigation program would reimburse a homeowner for 75% of the cost of putting his home up on pilings. This would remove the houses from immediate danger, but storms could still continue to wash sand out from beneath their homes. Plum Islanders circulated a sardonic joke among themselves that soon they would have to row a boat to get out to their homes perched on spindly stilts. That might work in the Gulf of Mexico, but not in the teeth of a raging North Atlantic storm.

Most of Harry's neighbors were planning to apply for permits to rebuild to keep their options open. But as they tallied up all the additional costs of rebuilding it started to make less and less sense. Five or six homeowners had already looked into the federal buyout program that would reimburse them for the fair market value of their homes from before hurricane Sandy. It made sense for the homeowners to apply now, because if they did nothing, the next time they applied they might only be eligible to be reimbursed for the value of their empty lot.

The problem with both programs is that there was a lot of time and paperwork involved. The state had only been given $7 Million dollars to distribute competitively to people that applied through their towns. Then FEMA had to decide if a house was in enough of an erosional hotspot to make the benefit of buying a house outweigh the costs of rebuilding it after every storm. The board of selectmen had to then decide if the town wanted to purchase the property. Finally the proposal would have to go before town meeting to see if taxpayers would be willing to pay 25% of the cost of a house in order to make a park out of the empty lot. But who would want to pay for a piece of property that was going to wash away anyway?

For the meantime however, Harry was pleased with the site visit. His engineers would have to supply information to the state on how high he expected to elevate his house, and more importantly, show that the remaining land on his property was still high enough to prevent the ocean from flowing through this island in the next significant storm, expected to arrive in the coming ten months.

Driftwood.

CHAPTER 23
THE BROMANCE
May 28, 2013

It was a cold drizzly day in late May when Governor Christie and Barack Obama rekindled the bromance they started in the ruins of Hurricane Sandy. Then, it was the last week of the presidential election and both Governor Romney and President Obama had managed to avoid that dreaded third rail topic, global warming. Then Hurricane Sandy destroyed his state and Governor Christie switched from being the Republican Party's pit bull attacking the President at every whistle stop, to Obama's most ardent admirer.

While Governor Romney was saying that global warming had nothing to do with Sandy and that FEMA's responsibilities should all be handed over to states, Christie was giving his newly beloved president bear hugs and saying what an "outstanding," "wonderful," even "excellent," job he was doing responding to New Jersey's crisis.

It drove the Republicans nuts. They had been trying to paint Obama as the anti-Christ and all they had done was make themselves look small. If there was one thing Governor Christie couldn't do, it was make himself look small.

The grand poobahs of the GOP were tone deaf to the concept of rising above politics. Didn't Christie know they had an election to win? The Conservative caucus was so incensed with the Governor of New Jersey that they disinvited him to their annual get together in Washington D.C. His mistake? He had requested too much money from Washington and had been successful at getting it to rebuild his state. Funny, most folks thought that was exactly what a governor was supposed to do.

Now, seven months later both men could use some of their former glow. Governor Christie was up for reelection and Barack Obama was being criticized for his handling of Benghazi, Libya, IRS, NSA, the Justice department, and eavesdropping on journalists.

Governor Christie and Barack Obama

Their big day started off with an unannounced stroll down New Jersey's Point Pleasant Boardwalk where the president tried to win a teddy bear by throwing a football through a tire. But after five perfect spirals and five perfect misses, the president seemed to be headed for what the New York Times termed, another one of his "public athletic calamities," including botched free throws at the White House basketball court, throwing a horrifyingly ugly first pitch at the Washington Nationals opening game and displaying bowling incompetence and ungainly form in the Pennsylvania Primaries.

Before the situation spiraled totally out of control, Governor Teddy Bear stepped up, grabbed a rubber football and tossed a wobbly pass just through the tire. For just a split second a   competitive smirk crossed his face, and he danced on his toes crowing "one and done, one and done!" Ever graceful under fire, President Obama turned, smiled and gave Christie an official high five POSTUS handshake – just like two twenty something year olds out on a post Memorial Day lark.

But at Ashbury Park things grew more serious. Obama pointed out that FEMA had been on the ground before Sandy struck, and would be there until everything was cleaned up. The governor was a quick read as well. After Sandy struck he had been famously quoted as saying he didn't know anything about climate change because he had been too busy doing other things. Since then he had entirely bought in to the need for government agencies like FEMA.

While the emphasis was on rebuilding what was less apparent were the long-term changes on the coasts. Nature was winning, for every house that was being rebuilt many more had been demolished or simply abandoned. Nature was seeing that the coast was becoming more resilient by permanently removing many of the houses that should never have been built on the barrier beaches in the first place.

The same thing had been true in Miami after Hurricane Andrew and in New Orleans after Katrina.

Another trend had been poor people swept away by rich people or more often by rich corporations. This had also been true after the 2004 tsunami where hundreds of thousands of fishermen were displaced off beaches to make way for hotels and casinos.

In New Jersey people were concerned about the same thing and claimed that mafia money was often behind the new resorts and that the owners didn't care if their hotel washed away after only a few years because they were using them to launder money anyway.

Could such a thing happen on Plum Island? Some claimed it already had in some of the nightclubs and intimate lounges on nearby Salisbury Beach.

Horseshoe Crabs

CHAPTER 24
" THE LIFE YOU SAVE MAY BE YOUR OWN. "
May 29, 2013

Pat Coren held the red knot in the palm of her hand while Larry
Niles put a shiny new band on its slender leg. This robin-sized
shorebird had just flown 5,400 miles from the tip of South America
to Delaware Bay. Pat let the bird go and it flew back to its flock
mates. Tomorrow night they would start the second non-stop leg
of their migration to the tundra high above the Arctic Circle.

The 40,000 tons of horseshoe crabs eggs the birds had consumed in the past two weeks would fuel their flight and provide
them with the fat they needed to allow them to start laying eggs
as soon as they landed. This was crucial to their reproductive success because snow would still be on the ground in the Arctic and
the insects they needed to survive would have not yet hatched.
Besides, this summer food lacked the high concentration of lipids
the red knots needed to produce their eggs.

It was awe inspiring that this quivering little ball of feathers
could make such a trip. Pat was proud that she had helped make
it happen. But this migration had almost not happened.

Hurricane Sandy had threatened to wipe out almost an entire
species of endangered bird because eighty percent of all the red
knots in the world time their migrations so they are the spawning
beaches of Delaware Bay when the horseshoe crabs are laying
their eggs. The birds are wholly dependent on horseshoe crab
eggs to fuel their migration, and the horseshoe crabs are wholly
dependent on the beaches of Delaware Bay that Sandy had just
washed away.

Both populations could have slipped over the edge but it hadn't happened because a coalition of scientists, volunteers, and environmental organizations had been counting the numbers of red knots and spawning horseshoe crabs for over thirty years. They were not going to let all that work go down the drain.

They had raised over a million dollars and removed 40 tons of bulkheads and concrete rubble. These were the remains of anti-erosion devices that had actually sped up the rate of erosion.

They had profiled the beach and measured the size of its grains before spreading 50 truckloads of new sand along this mile of beach. Federal, state and town agencies had all streamlined their permitting procedures so the work could be completed in time so the early spring tides could aerate and winnow down the beach before the horseshoe crabs arrived on the late May tides.

The results had been far beyond expectations. Hundreds of thousands of horseshoe crabs had laid untold tons of horseshoe crab eggs. Hundreds of thousands of red knots, ruddy turnstones and laughing gulls had all gorged on the bounty, then arrived on their nesting grounds fat, happy and ready to breed. The beach had even been improved from what it had been before the storm.

It had been a wildly unexpected environmental success. But it had also been a medical success. Processed horseshoe crab blood is worth over $15,000 a quart. It is used to test for Gram-negative bacteria. Anything that comes in contact with the human blood system whether it be a syringe, scalpel or flu vaccine has to be tested to be sure that it is free of Gram-negative bacteria and Gram-negative bacteria are as lethal as they are ubiquitous in the warm shallow waters where horseshoe crabs thrive.

The ancient animals have devised a unique strategy to protect themselves from this class of bacteria. If a human gets a wound we have about 20 different kinds of immune cells to fight the infection. But horseshoe crabs only have a single kind of amoebic cell that migrates to the wound and coagulates to keep the infection out.

It is a primitive immune system but it has protected horseshoe crabs for over 400 million years, way before there were birds, fish, and dinosaurs, to say nothing of humans on this earth. The bottom line is that the human health system is critically dependent on this single species of wild animal that lives up and down the East Coast from Maine to Florida.

But horseshoe crabs have been declining throughout their range because they are also used as bait to catch eels and conch used in the sushi industry. If the crabs are kept alive to be used for the medical industry each crab is worth about $2,500. If they are chopped up and used for bait they are worth about 30 cents a pound.

Delaware Bay has the largest crabs and the largest population of crabs on the East Coast. If this population had crashed it would have affected the health of millions of humans all over the world. Instead this turned out to be one Hurricane Sandy's most heartening stories of recovery. Pat was proud she had played a small part in the effort.

Teens Lounging on a Groin

CHAPTER 25
GROINS ON A BEACH
May 30, 2013

A few days after the site visit, I went on Google Earth to get an image of how high Plum Island was near Harry Trout's house. You can do this by flying the camera all the way down to sea level than taking a picture of the island from across the water. I had discovered this trick when I was writing about shrimp fishing in the Gulf of Mexico and wanted to see what it would look like if you were on one of the fifty odd boats jockeying for position at night in the inward rushing tidal currents between the offshore islands.

But what struck me most about the Plum Island image was that all the lost houses had been sitting just north of rock groins that jutted out perpendicularly from the beach. The groins had been installed between 1962 and 1965, to protect houses on the southern side of the groins.

There are a lot of problems with groins on a beach, just think of Burt Lancaster and Deborah Kerr rolling around in the surf in "From Here to Eternity." But the problem with rock groins is that they do a good job of protecting houses on the upstream side of the beach, but they increase the amount of erosion on the downstream side.

The evidence of this was dramatic. On Plum Island, Jeanne's abandoned restaurant and the Buzzotta house had been just downstream of the Center groin. The Fordham Way houses had been just downstream of the Fordham Way groin and the Annapolis Way houses had been downstream of the Annapolis Way groin. In all nine houses had been destroyed just downstream of groins.

Three houses were lost just downstream of each groin
Google Earth

It is interesting that when the groins were built people realized that sand flowed south to north on this part of the beach. But the Army Corps of Engineers changed that perception when they were brought in to fix the Merrimack River jetties. The Corps wanted to get the contract so they started to circulate the idea that water flowing out of the Merrimack River created a current that carried sand north to south. It had been a convenient idea because it allowed them to make their cost benefit analysis work.

The idea that there was an a south flowing offshore current had become more and more entrenched in local knowledge until people were convinced that this current was so powerful that it built up a two mile long underwater sandbar that had caused hot spots of erosion to move down the beach as it grew.

But the simpler explanation that works on every other barrier beach on the East Coast is that sand washes off the beach during the winter when the energy is high and is stored offshore in underwater patches of well-dispersed sand. Then, when the season changes, lower energy, longer period waves bunch that sand up into sandbars that are visible at low tide. These transverse bars then become oblique bars as they attach to the shore. This gives the appearance that a powerful current has built a two-mile long underwater sandbar offshore; instead waves have just pushed a series of individual sandbars toward the beach all summer.

But many prominent people had told me that this south flowing current existed so I didn't doubt its existence but I did doubt that repairing the Merrimack River jetty would make a particle of difference to the houses on the Fordham and Annapolis streets two miles away. Almost 30 homes were still condemned there as well, so they would also be more vulnerable than last year to the coming winter's fast approaching storms.

Winter is fast approaching.

Preparing to rebuild on exactly the same footprint as before.

CHAPTER 26
LAWSUITS AND LEGALITIES
June 4, 2013

A few weeks after Harry's site visit the state backed down. People only heard about it when Bob Connors wrote a letter to several homeowners saying that the Department of Environmental Protection had withdrawn its intervention. If it were true it would mean that Harry Trout and his neighbors would be able to rebuild their houses on almost the same footprint as before.

But nobody seemed to know the real story. The DEP made it clear that the intervention was in progress. One of their spokesmen indicated the action might have been initiated in another sector of the Department of Energy and Environmental Affairs.

The truth was, Bob had been very busy. He sat on the board of the Pacific Legal Foundation. It was the country's oldest and most successful right wing legal organization, funded by the Koch brothers, the oil and tobacco industries, and the Scaife Foundation. It had been established by a group of lawyers working for then California District Attorney General Ed Meese and Governor Reagan to counter welfare reform and target environmental groups like the Sierra Club and the Environmental Defense Fund.

In 1991, the Phillip Morris tobacco company had bailed out the Pacific Legal Foundation financially, then used the foundation to enlist think tanks like the Hoover Institute to write OPED pieces attacking the EPA's determination that tobacco smoke causes cancer.

But the legal foundation's main business had always been to support anti-environmental cases. Their early work involved actions advocating for the use of DDT, for using herbicides in national forests and for using public lands for range without requiring environmental impact reviews. They had also supported 6 pro-nuclear power plant cases and by 1998 were receiving more than $110,000 a year from Exxon Mobil.

In the 1980's the Pacific Legal Foundation won several coastal property rights cases stemming from the Supreme Court ruling that any environmental regulation that lowered the value of someone's property could be considered a "taking" under the 5th amendment. That meant that a town or state enforcing such a law could be required to reimburse a homeowner, or more likely a developer, for the full value of his property.

Ken Kimmel knew how powerful the Pacific Legal Foundation was. The head of the Massachusetts DEP had gone to law school at UCLA. He took one look at the foundation's e-mail threatening to sue and had decided to back down. The letter had also gone to Newbury's town administrator Tracy Blais.

A few nights later the chairman of the board of selectmen Joe Story was on television with Bob Connors and Harry Trout demanding that the DEP official who had made the inspection be fired -- the state employee's fault? He had put two conditions on Harry's order to rebuild. One, that he would not be able to build any bulkheads, revetments or seawalls, and two he would have to assume responsibility for the risk of shoreline erosion.

The state analyst had used mainstream science to determine that if Harry built a new coastal engineering structure it would only hasten the demise of his neighbor's property. That is exactly what had happened to six of the houses that had toppled into the surf. They had all been built downstream of bulkheads, groins and sea-walls. The most massive bulkhead had belonged to Harry Trout and it had arguably caused his two neighbors to lose their houses.

If the DEP did decide to let Harry off the hook, it would be no skin off the state officials' noses if the rebuilt houses washed away. The officials were essentially throwing up their hands and saying "let nature run its course".

So the homeowners had won every battle; free rein to scrape and mine the beach, free rein to build illegal seawalls and artificial sand dunes and free rein to rebuild houses on the same footprint as before.

The homeowners had won all the human battles. But, had they just set themselves up for losing the war against mother nature?

If homeowners wanted to spend their own money fighting such pyrrhic battles that was their right and their own concern. But should taxpayers be required to pay for homeowner's folly by subsidizing the Federal Flood Insurance Program to reimburse homeowners again and again to rebuild their homes?

That issue was due to arise in June when FEMA was scheduled to present its new flood plain maps. Would maps reflect that Harry and his neighbors had a one percent chance of flooding again? If so, it would drive their insurance rates higher and require them to add on another $30,000 to $40,000 to the cost of elevating and rebuilding their already expensive homes.

CHAPTER 27
MICHAEL BLOOMBERG
Manhattan Island June 11, 2013

Mayor Bloomberg mused as he approached the Brooklyn Navy Yard. His had been a career path taken by far too many New Englanders -- hone your skills in Boston then go for the big bucks in New York. At least Pedro Martinez had the decency to join the Mets instead of the Yankees.

Michael's trajectory had included growing up in Medford Massachusetts, building up the eponymously named Bloomberg News Network then, rather curiously, running for Mayor of the Big Apple.

Now he wanted to use the last days of his unprecedented 3rd term in office to do something about climate change. And in New York fashion he wanted to do it big and expensive -- $20 billion dollars big, and $20 billion dollars expensive. As difficult as it is for a New Englander to admit, New York also had the bucks to do it right.

Hurricane Sandy had been a wake-up call for the mayor as it had been for his neighbor across the river, Governor Christie. Like Christie he wanted to make preparing for the next big storm the signature issue of his final days in office.

His aides had already prepared the press. Yesterday they released figures that showed that by 2050 up to a quarter of the city's land area would be living within the 100-year floodplain. That meant that if the city did nothing, more than 40 miles of waterfront containing 800,000 New Yorkers would be experiencing flooding during regular high tides and significantly more days with nine-ty-degree weather. Of course he couldn't resist pointing out that 800,000 people was many more people than live in Minneapolis.

Today he was going to announce his $20 billion dollar plan to protect the city, and tomorrow he was going to announce his plan to totally redo the city's building code in light of future natural disasters.

With luck, the following day would find him playing golf on his favorite course on Bermuda. He flew out to his second island home so often in his private corporate jet that many of the snark-ier members of the New York City Press had started referring to his Tucker's Town home as the city's second City Hall, and Ber-muda as New York's missing 6th borough.

Of course everyone in Massachusetts knows that New York's missing borough is not missing at all. It is Dukes County in Mas-sachusetts that includes Martha's Vineyard and Nantucket. They only look like New York when the tourists arrive every summer.

The Brooklyn Navy Yard was a fitting setting for the mayor's presentation. He opened his speech by explaining that in the 1940's the yard had been nicknamed the "Can Do Yard" because it exemplified the spirit and resolve of the wartime city saying. "Today this building that once turned out battleships, is now helping us lead another battle, the battle against climate change."

He explained that his administration hadn't waited for Washing-ton to lead on climate change but had attacked the problem head-on as many other cities were doing.

But Hurricane Sandy had made it clear that no matter how far the city had come it still had a long way to go and he reminded his audience that as bad as Sandy had been, future storms could be even worse. Because of warmer water temperatures and sea level rise, in 20 or 40 years even a smaller storm could be more destructive than Sandy. Hurricane Sandy caused $19 Billion and if nothing were done by 2050 a storm that size would cost five times more, about $90 Billion dollars. Now he was talking real money.

"As New Yorkers, I believe we cannot and will not abandon our waterfront. It is one of our greatest assets and we have worked too hard to bring it back. We must protect it, not retreat from it!"

He started by looking at the city's first line of defense, the natural systems that had attracted the early Dutch settlers in the first place. He showed before and after shots of the 94th Street Beach in the Rockaways and the 56 Street Beach just two miles away. The first beach had had no dunes and been washed away by the storm.

"The second beach had a strong natural dune system and had mostly survived The combination of natural dunes and wide beaches with ample sand is a potent one."

He proposed building a double dune system in Breezy Point that would eventually be extended across the Rockaways. He went on to enumerate 37 other coastal defense projects including restoring natural wetlands and building a breakwater on Staten Island's Great Kills Harbor.

He described small affordable storm surge barriers that would prevent back door flooding and Blue Belts that had been effective in absorbing floodwaters in Staten Island during the storm. He promised to work with the Army Corps of Engineers on its $20 Million study of flood protection possibilities across the entire Northeastern seaboard.

Finally he pointed out that Battery Park City had done much to protect inland areas on the Lower West Side and that a proposed new city called Seaport City could do the same thing for Manhattan's Lower East Side.

He ended by saying, "This is New York City. We've always turned challenges into opportunities. Sandy was a temporary setback that can ultimately propel us forward, if we think big and seize the moment."

Now there was a politician that knew his audience, those damn Yankees had done it again!

CHAPTER 28
THE LEGACY ISSUE
June 25, 2013

President Obama laid out his plan to address global warming on a typically sweltering hot Washington day in late June. He acknowledged the heat by taking off his jacket to the cheers of hundreds of rowdy coeds spread out on Georgetown University's grassy campus. "It's not all that sexy," winked the President.

It was a fitting opening to America's long awaited plan to address the planet's most all-encompassing crisis. The President had pledged to do something about climate change in his 2008 presidential campaign, but after the election Senate Republicans had shot down his global warming bill so he switched his focus to reforming health care and reviving the economy—the economy that President Bush had left on palliative care only.

But Obama's advisors figured out that there was a lot they could without congressional approval. The EPA dramatically increased new car fuel efficiency and promulgated the first-ever rules on the emissions of green house gasses from power plants.

But global warming became too hot to handle during Obama's campaign for a second term. Curbing coal use was mentioned as little as possible in the swing vote, coal-producing states of Ohio, Pennsylvania and West Virginia.

But Hurricane Sandy had put the issue back on the front burner during the final days of the campaign and Obama made climate change one of the focal points of his second inaugural address. He featured the issue again when the world's eyes were on him in Berlin.

So Obama admitted to his Georgetown audience that action on climate change had been a long time in coming. He cleverly pointed out that scientists had first become alarmed about the build-up of carbon dioxide back when the United States started going into space. That was well before most of his audience had even been born.

He reeled off figures about the present situation, 2012 had been the hottest year on record, it had tornadoes, forest fires and the worst drought since the Dust Bowl. And then it had ended with Hurricane Sandy.

"In a world that is warmer than it used to be, all weather events are affected by a warmer climate. These are demonstrable facts. The overwhelming judgment of science, of chemistry and physics, has put the argument to rest. The planet is warming and human activity is contributing to it."

He reminded his audience that the Clean Air Act had been enacted under the Nixon Administration and passed both the house and the Senate with only one dissenting vote.

"We don't know who that guy is. I haven't had time to do the research to figure it out, yet." He paused theatrically to wipe the sweat off his brow as another carbon dioxide spewing jet flew low overhead from the nearby Ronald Reagan airport. The genial 40th president had done more to turn back the clock on fixing global warming than any other man on the planet.

Obama explained that the EPA was now mandated to curtail carbon dioxide emission from power plants because the courts had ruled that the potent green gas was also a pollutant. He pointed out that, "We had no choice in 1957, and we have no choice now. We have to put an end to the limitless dumping of carbon pollution out of power plants."

"Now coal companies and polluters will say this proposal is a job killer. How do I know? Because that is what they say every time! Those who think the economy cant adjust have a fundamental lack of faith in American business and American ingenuity." His statement signaled the eventual demise of the coal industry. It was an antiquated fuel that should have been outlawed by Nixon's Clean Air Act, back in 1972.

He worked his audience into a final lather by promising that his administration would do something he admitted it hadn't really done before, assume a leadership role in the international fight to combat climate change.

"We don't have time for another meeting of the Flat Earth Society. Sticking your head in the sand might make you feel safer but it wont save you from the next storm."

The President closed by dropping an unexpected bombshell. He announced that the $7 billion Keystone pipeline would not be permitted to pass if the net effect of the pipeline would significantly exacerbate the problem of carbon pollution. That was pretty much a slam-dunk proposition. If the pipeline went through it would carry oil extracted from the dirty tar sands of Alberta to the smoky refineries of Texas. Every step of the way would produce far more carbon dioxide than producing natural gas or drilling for oil.

But by this time all the major networks had switched back to their regular programming, only the weather channel was still faithfully broadcasting what could prove to be the most far reaching speech of our century.

But the young audience at Georgetown University had heard their president's message loud and clear. Their applause drowned out his final summation. They knew they might have just heard one of the most important speeches in our planet's hopefully long history.

Building a new house in the primary dune.

CHAPTER 29
THE BUILDER
June 27, 2013

Tom Gorenflo loved to watch Eddie Boyle's excavator drive the long steel pilings deep into the dunes overlooking the Atlantic Ocean. Each pulse of the vibratory hammer on the far end of the excavator arm pushed another piling several more feet into the soft sand.

Their plan was to drive 17 of these main pilings thirty to thirty-five feet below grade then build a brand new house on top of that sturdy but spindly looking foundation. The March storm had damaged an outbuilding on the lot, but the owner had already decided to tear down its old summer cottage and replace it with a larger, year-round building with one the best ocean views in the world.

This was the 15th house Tom had built on Plum Island. He did good work and didn't need to advertise. Most of his jobs came through word of mouth from satisfied customers. Plus, Tom was a nice thoughtful guy. He was quick to point out that he was certainly not an environmentalist but that he also knew that, "you can't just do whatever you want out here."

He knew this from experience. He had lived and worked in four of the East Coast's erosional hotspots. He had grown up and gone to high school in New Jersey, spent two long seasons on Martha's Vineyard, then moved to Florida where he had learned the building trade.

For the past 27 years Tom had lived and worked on Plum Island, but he always made sure his house was several blocks back from the primary dune. "Frankly, where I live now, I'm more concerned by flooding coming in from the backside of the island than from the ocean side."

But Tom also knew why homeowners on Plum Island wanted to rebuild. He loved the beauty of the island with its expansive ocean beach and extensive backside marshes. Plum Island was more like the islands of the Outer Banks and like those islands it was rapidly eroding. But Tom was willing to put up with the risk of erosion in exchange for the privilege of living on this unique piece of real estate.

"You have to look at history. The reason the North End of Plum Island is so crowded is that most of the houses out there were originally on the outer beach. They were mostly old fishing shacks so it didn't really matter. You just moved them onto your cousin's property, so you finally ended up with having lots of houses doubled up in crowded island lots."

"That guy on out on Annapolis Way, Milton Tzitzenikos, has the ability to do that. His house is already up on skids ready to be moved. His lot extends across the street. If I were him I'd also move it over there."

But most of the people who lived in the 39 homes that had been severely damaged in the winter didn't have that choice. It was already summer and very few of them had elevated their homes or done anything else to prepare them for the upcoming stormy season.

Tom hoped that the erosion would reverse itself on Plum Island but he was also a realist, "We could have another bad winter and the people out there might just be out of luck."

Tom had just returned from a fishing trip to Martha's Vineyard where he had seen more results of the past winter's storms. "We watched a crew move a multi-million dollar mansion with an in-ground swimming pool and bowling alley back from the edge of a rapidly eroding cliff." It had given him pause. He knew they would probably just have to move the house again.

"When I went first went there in 1972 you never saw that kind of money. Now you see it all over the coast. I guess people need to be near the water."

The worst storm Tom had ever experienced was the so-called "Perfect Storm" in 1992. "I was wading around in knee-deep water and saw at least three two--foot high waves roll down Jackson Way and into the marsh."

The waves scoured concrete blocks out of people's foundations in the low spot at the end of Fordham Way and destroyed a house on Annapolis Way – a house that had only been two or three years old.

Tom had never experienced what it felt like to put a year of your life into building a home and then have to watch as it tumbled into the ocean.

He knew that the pilings would protect the new house they were building, but he also knew there was nothing you could do to prevent storms from washing away the sand underneath a house. "Like everyone else, I hope that the erosion will reverse itself like it has in the past, but I dunno."

I asked Tom what he would do if someone asked him to build a house he didn't think would last. He felt that people had a right to do whatever they wanted with their own land and their own money. It was their own business.

He could also vouch for his own building skills, but he wouldn't make any false promises about how long he felt the dune under the house might last. "I would probably tell him it wasn't a good idea to build...They are just sandbars out there, and sandbars are always moving."

This brand new house was built 50 feet from the ocean edge.

A small group of committed people

CHAPTER 30
"STORM SURGE"
July 1, 2013

It was already the beginning of July before I had a chance to return to Plum Island. It was on a fittingly stormy night. Fierce winds
beat a tattoo of raindrops on my windshield as I drove through the
bucolic towns of Ipswich, Rowley and Newbury. The radio warned
of coastal flooding and tornadoes. But everything seemed to mag-
ically stop as I approached the headquarters of the Parker River
National Wildlife Refuge.

A young woman wearing a University of Maryland tee shirt led
a bedraggled group into an executive suite where they took seats
around a much too plush conference table. I'm not sure it was
what Margaret Mead had in mind when she talked about a small
group of committed individuals, but it was an awfully nice place to
hammer out the details of the first working storm surge group in
America.

Someone had asked me to join this group, forming to look at
the effects of sea level rise on places like Plum Island. Against my
better judgment I had agreed. Did I want to cross that inviolate
line that separates the participant from the observer? Who was I
kidding? I had crossed that line several years before.

The outreach committee had selected the term "Storm Surge
Workgroup" because they felt it neatly tied together the coastal
concerns of people on Plum Island with those who lived on the
shorelines and floodplains of the Merrimack River Valley.

People on Plum Island and in the Merrimack River Valley were governed by disparate state and town entities but all of them were getting used to being inundated by storms battering the island and surging down the Merrimack River.

They also felt that the concept neatly avoided the old time consuming arguments about sea level rise, climate change and whether or not they are caused by human activities. I said that I found that as soon as you mentioned the words "sea level rise" or "climate change" you lost half your audience. But everybody believes in storms and most people believe they have become more intense and more frequent in recent years.

The group also felt that a storm surge committee could fill in a gap in the regulatory system. You had towns that made decisions about things like zoning laws and where you could build a house, and you had state agencies that regulated the coasts and river valleys. But there were very few groups that concerned themselves with the common problems of both regions threatened by storms and sea level rise.

By the end of the night the outreach committee convinced the hub of people who had started the group that it made more sense to establish a Storm Surge group that could go out and engage the public, than a sea level rise group that would be simply preaching to the choir.

But it had been a long night. It seemed like the system of technical sub-committees reporting to a central decision making body, a so-called Hub and spoke structure, made more sense for a large corporation or group of governmental collaborators than to a small group of volunteers.

But that would be a battle for another night. The committee was satisfied that they had just established probably the first working storm surge group ever. Perhaps it would even become a model for similar groups assembling up and down the East Coast in the wake of Hurricane Sandy.

Sargassum weed, Galveston, Texas

CHAPTER 31
SEAWEED AND SAND DUNES
July 8, 2013

It is early morning on Galveston's East Beach. A lone jogger runs through the shallow waters and beach goers set up umbrellas so they can sit in the shade, but still catch the onshore breezes blowing off the tepid waters of the Gulf of Mexico. It is going to be another hot, steamy day on Galveston Island.

But there is a problem out here. Last night's "bull tide" deposited 50 acres of Sargassum weed on the beach. Now it glistens in the morning sun emitting an ungodly odor. It is the smell of iodine and vegetative decay -- the stench of death itself. Bulldozers have been hard at work since dawn pushing the seaweed into piles of rotting vegetation. But it is an expensive proposition keeping Texas beaches free of this common problem.

Sargassum weed is normally found rooted in the shallow waters of the Caribbean, but it can also break free and float to the surface buoyed by its multitude of small gas filled bladders. It can then survive on the surface for months at a time, but a lot of it dies off in the pale blue, nutrient poor waters of the Atlantic.

But if currents happen to carry the weed into the nutrient rich green waters of the Gulf of Mexico, it will blossom into long windrows of yellowish vegetation that can stretch across the surface for several hundred miles. The blooms are further enhanced by the steady stream of fertilizers that run off the agricultural fields of the South and mid-west and on into the many major rivers that flow into the Gulf from Texas to Florida.

Sargassum weed is such a problem, that Captain Robert Webster of Texas A&M has made a career of using images from spotter planes and satellites to make daily forecasts of when massive patches of the seaweed will land on Texas beaches.

But there is another problem on Galveston Island; a reminder of it sits on the beach further west. It is a 17-foot high seawall that stretches for several miles across the city's waterfront. The expensive structure was built after the 1900 Galveston Hurricane caused the worst natural disaster in American history.

Prior to the storm, Galveston had been the fourth largest city in Texas, also boasting the state's highest per capita income. She had just surpassed New Orleans as the nation's largest exporter of cotton and was behind only New York in exports of wheat.

Galveston was also a fashionable summer resort where people came from cities like Dallas and Houston to escape the inland heat. She hosted a busy social season that revolved around a demanding dance card of picnics, concerts, balls and bicycle races, many of them held on the cool wide strand of Galveston's many beaches.

In fact everyone did their level best to ignore the inconvenient truth that they lived in one of the most hurricane prone areas in the world, on a 30-mile long barrier beach whose highest elevation was only nine feet above sea level. It inspired about as much confidence as living twenty feet below the sea in nearby New Orleans.

In fact, Galveston was so low that only a fair to middling sized New England high tide, the kind of you might see any month on Plum Island, would have been more than enough to flood the entire city of thirty-seven thousand people.

But everything changed on September 8, 1900. People had been lounging on the broad verandas of Tremont Hotel or strolling along the city's beaches that were so wide that they often held automobile races on them at low tide.

But by late afternoon a rising wind started to push waves into the Gulf side streets, however nobody paid much attention. They knew the water would just drain back into the ocean. Everyone had lived through hurricanes before. Why should they leave the safety of their own homes? Why risk getting caught on the single narrow congested causeway that led off the island?

By early evening the bay waters and gulf waters merged in the center of the island so the city was already underwater when the full fury of storm hit at 6 PM. Thirty-foot waves riding on top of a record high storm surge knocked Gulf side houses off their foundations, then used them as battering rams to knock down the next line of homes.

Survivors heard the cries of their family members and neighbors as they were swept down streets and out into the Gulf of Mexico, where many were eaten by sharks. By the end of the fearful night between 6,000 and 10,000 people, almost a third of the island's population, had either been drowned or crushed to death in the maelstrom of heavy debris.

The following day Captain Thornton sailed down Galveston Bay to look for survivors, but the water was so full of floating corpses that they made an unsettling sound as they bumped and scraped against his hull. He finally sent a crew member armed with a pike to the bow to push the cadavers out of his way.

A year later, Galveston came up with an audacious plan to bring the city back to life. It was the progressive era and people thought anything could be done using science and technology.

They used human powered jackscrews to elevate every house, hotel and hospital 17 feet up into the air. Then they sent barges down special canals cut into the island. The barges sprayed a slurry of sand and water dredged from the nearby Gulf under each building, until the entire center of the city had been raised 17 feet.

Finally the city raised $1.6 Million dollars, an astronomical sum in those days, to build the 17-foot high seawall. The entire project took twelve years to complete. During that time people had to navigate over the streets of Galveston using a rickety system of raised catwalks to avoid the slough of sand and muddy brown water.

The seawall received its first major test when another hurricane struck in 1915. Almost all the structures behind the wall were saved, but after the storm passed, people noticed that the beach was gone. The storm's high-energy waves had washed it completely out to sea. Ever since, Galveston has had to spend the equivalent of several seawalls every few decades to pump ever more sand onto its beaches.

But in 2013 another Texas A&M professor, Jens Filgus, came up with an ingenious plan to use one problem to solve another. He convinced the city of Galveston to spend $140,000 to use its troublesome Sargassum weed to fortify a system of sand dunes as its first line of defense to protect the city against future hurricanes.

He used water tank experiments to show that while a single sand dune of loosely consolidated sand would actually increase the rate of erosion; a natural sand dune system with a foreshore berm and sand dune behind it could significantly reduce the rate of erosion. If you fortified the berm with seaweed its water content would make the berm more compact and its organics would fertilize the growth of stabilizing dune vegetation.

AP picked up the story and it was featured in papers across the country. It arrived just in time for a small group of homeowners on Plum Island. They had been working on their own plan to rebuild an artificial sand dune that had been thrown together after the 1978 Blizzard. It had somehow lasted for 35 years with only four repairs. As sometimes happens, the beach had also been in one of its natural erosional pauses during that period of years.

The homeowners planned to present their plan for a single sand dune on July 19th but the thought occurred to many that if you are going to build an artificial sand dune you might as well do it right...

A beachside interview with Senator Tarr.

CHAPTER 32
THE SENATOR
July 15, 2013

The first time I met Bruce Tarr he was riding an all terrain vehicle hell bent for leather down Plum Island Beach. He had just received word that homeowners had been given permission to install Geotubes and he wanted to give Bob Connors the good news.

Bruce loved being in the midst of the fray; taking calls, giving interviews, making decisions. His website pointed out that the young senator had a passion for constituent services. But he didn't just have a passion for constituent services; he was constituent service on steroids. I had seen him on the beach so many times last winter I started to wonder when he ever had a chance to legislate.

But he must have been pretty good at it. The young Republican was Senate Minority leader although he sometimes sounded like a bleeding heart Liberal:

"My lowest day out there was when Mrs. Buzzotta's house was torn down. Its just indescribable how gut wrenching that experience is. It didn't like standing there with no answers."

But the Senator's highest day came when he finally sat down at the Old Newbury Country Club with Ron Barrett from the Plum Island Tax Payers Association and Bob Connors from the Plum Island Foundation. PITA represented the old guard on the island who remembered the days when they referred to themselves as

Slum Islanders. The Foundation represented the wealthy new comers who had built homes after the sewer and water were installed.

They had been discussing having Essex County buy its own dredge so it could maintain its own rivers and harbors. But eventually they realized that a dredge big enough to operate in the Merrimack River would be too large to operate in smaller waterways like the Ipswich, Essex and Annisquam rivers. Besides it was just too damn expensive to own and operate your own barge. It made much more sense to get the Army Corps of Engineers to do the dredging for you.

"But I made the point that if we were going to succeed in convincing the Corps to dredge the Merrimack River, everyone had to be sitting around the same table. So perhaps against my better judgment, I was drawn into the idea of forming the Merrimack River Beach Alliance."

The Senator's second best day was when he convinced the state Department of Conservation and Recreation to pay for Geotubes, the sand-filled tubes made of coconut fiber to protect people's houses north of Plum Island's Center Island.

The problem was, none of these costly measures had really worked. Erosion was happening faster than ever, and almost a third of the houses on Annapolis and Fordham Ways were more vulnerable than before.

But, so far the various groups representing Plum Island had won all the human battles. They had convinced Congress to fund the Army Corps of Engineers to repair the Merrimack River jetties, they had received permission to anchor layers of three foot diameter Geotubes into the sand, they had received permission to scrape the beach to build a 40 foot artificial seawall, and they had even gotten away with illegally building rock seawalls without receiving the normal $40,000 fines from either the state or the Army Corps of Engineers.

Now Senator Tarr wanted to press the advantage by establishing a state commission to investigate the laws and regulations governing what homeowners could and couldn't do to fight erosion.

Perhaps the commission would recommend reorganizing the state's environmental agencies to get rid of the Department of Environmental Protection. Perhaps they would recommend rewriting the Wetlands Protection Act so it would be less frustrating for homeowners.

But the commission might also find that the present system was OK, or even suggest that the Commonwealth do more to discourage people from building on vulnerable places like Plum Island. But the Senator felt these were all risks worth taking. It had been a long time since the present laws and regulations had been enacted and it made sense to review how well they worked.

I asked the Senator how he could square spending so much money to slow erosion with the traditional fiscal conservatism of his party. Wouldn't it require huge outlays of public and private funds to thwart these forces of nature?

He answered with, "that's a very good question," but went on to explain that he felt it was important to protect the houses and infrastructure that were already there.

But he also knew that the Pacific Legal Foundation was planning to open a local office on the North Shore. They would be the heavy artillery for what many saw as the final showdown between erosion and homeowners' rights.

Of course I couldn't help but ask the obvious question, "Why not just pass a law making it illegal for any beach to erode in Massachusetts?"

He laughed good-naturedly. But it was time to move on to another constituent.

MRBA members in front of PITA Hall

CHAPTER 33
THE MRBA
July 19, 2013

It is a truth universally acknowledged that one opens any meeting in New England by first recognizing the weather. Bruce Tarr followed the injunction by thanking the Plum Island Taxpayer's Association for allowing the Merrimack River Beach Alliance to hold its annual mid-summer meeting in their way over air-conditioned PITA hall.

New Englanders aren't used to rushing from one air-conditioned building to another. It makes us feel housebound and grumpy. That is the sort of thing that retirees do in Arizona, not on Plum Beach where you should be enjoying the last few brief days of summer.

It is supposed to be the time when you would grill some burgers, enjoy the beach, dig some clams and go fishing. All the same, everyone seemed to be more than happy to be sitting in the air-conditioned hall. It sure beat sweltering in a Boston office or being trapped in a beach house without A/C.

My first impression of the meeting was how little had actually been accomplished since the winter storms. It was almost spooky on the beach. Tom Gorenflo and Eddie Boyle were about the only two people doing any construction work. I had expected to see dozens of contractors working all summer to prepare houses for the fast approaching storm season.

Most of the people who lost their homes had gone before the Newbury Conservation Commission but it had been primarily to beat the statue of limitations for applying to rebuild. Only two homeowners had actually gone through the entire process and received building permits from the town. It seemed like most people wanted to see what other homeowners were going to do, and more importantly, to figure out how much it was really going to cost to rebuild.

The storms had sped up the rate of gentrification on the island. The old timers didn't have the money to rebuild along the lines suggested by the state's Department of Environmental Protection. It would cost them $60,000 dollars to just drive in pilings to elevate their homes and as soon as they did so, they would lose their subsidized flood insurance.

Plus the Federal Emergency Management Agency had just released its new flood plain maps that had put many more people in the higher paying velocity zone. One Plum Islander testified that after the storms his grandfathered insurance rate had risen from only a few thousand dollars a year, to close to $500 a month.

Ron Barrett explained that most of his PITA constituents were retired blue-collar workers with limited funds. They couldn't afford to pay that amount of money to elevate their homes plus pay for higher insurance rates and mortgages, so they were looking at cheaper ways to deal with the problem.

That was the perfect cue for Senator Tarr to segue to the second major item on the agenda, beach mining. He turned to Marc Sarkady to explain the Plum Island Foundation's proposal to build an artificial sand dune to protect the 30-oceanfront homes on Annapolis and Fordham Ways.

It was essentially the same plan he had presented to the FEMA officials after the March storm. It called for using bulldozers to push sand off the beach at low tide, then pile it up into a ten-foot high sand dune that would be thirty feet deep and almost a quarter of a mile long. But it was essentially just a smaller version of the 40-foot high sand dune that had failed in October. They just called it beach mining now instead of beach scraping.

Numerous researchers like Jens Filgus had conducted studies that showed that such a simple man-made design would increase the rate of erosion, but that a dune that mimicked nature with a dune and an adjoining berm could significantly slow the rate of erosion. Theoretically, the berm would be washed away in a major storm, but the dune would remain to protect the houses behind it. However, the sacrificial berm would have to be replaced after every storm, so during a year like this past season, it would have cost almost $24,000 to build and repair such a dune system.

The foundation had originally hoped they could build the first phase of the sand dune in front of Bob Connors' home. He could certainly afford the initial $8,000 to pay for it, but the three houses on either side of him had tumbled into the surf and their owners hadn't applied for building permits. They were damned if they were going to shell out another $8,000 to protect their empty lots.

Marc admitted it was going to be a hard sell to convince home-owners who had already paid $40,000 to build an illegal seawall, to turn around and pay for a sacrificial sand dune, along with a new mortgage -- if they could get one. The area's largest local bank had stopped giving out mortgages to build houses on Plum Island, others were sure to follow.

But Ken Kimmel, the head of the state's DEP, grimacing from a bad back and stress over the situation, said he was encouraged by the project. "I have heard from island residents that it worked successfully in the past, so yes I am interested." That signaled that the Department of Environmental Protection knew that if they turned the proposal down the Pacific Legal Foundation would step in and sue the state claiming that such a move would be unconstitutional.

But the Army Corps of Engineers representatives were less intimidated. They said that their office would have to review the project along with Fish and Wildlife and the National Marine Fisheries Service. Their noses were still out of joint because the homeowners had gone ahead and built seawalls without the Corps' permission. The Corps had sent a letter to the homeowners and the town of Newbury threatening them all with $40,000 fines.

Although the meeting had been as quiet and amiable as a Jane Austen novel, it was clear that there were gaps and fissures simmering just below the surface. Would they erupt when the Alliance met privately next week?

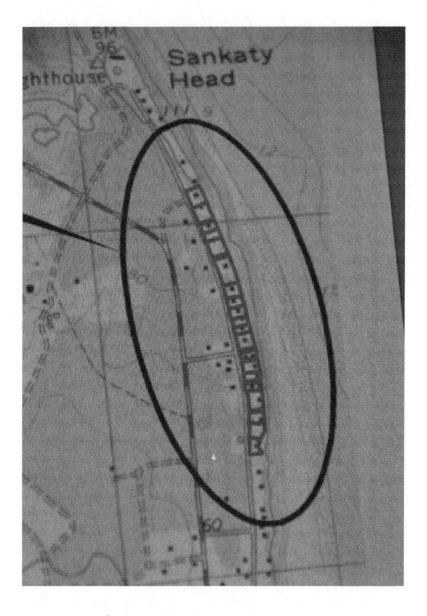

"I've lived on Sconset all my life, never been to Nantucket though."
-Old time Sconset resident

CHAPTER 34
SIASCONSET
July 24, 2013

In 2006 I took my family on a busman's holiday to Nantucket Is-land. We stayed in a delightful little summer cottage only fifty feet from the beach. But it gradually dawned on me that my affinity for this place was the crux of the problem. People are drawn to the edge of the ocean; the closer to the mist and sounds of the crash-ing waves the better. But while this cottage was the first place you would want to rent, it was the last place you would want to own.

The cottage was in Codfish Park. A neat little community of fifty cottages nestled below Sconset Bluffs. On a beautiful summer day it seemed like the perfect place to buy. In fact the converted barn was for sale for close to a million dollars. Out of curiosity I called the broker, who extolled the virtues of the unique communi-ty.

But what she failed to mention was that in 1992, fifteen of these cottages had been swept away by the Perfect Storm. The Weath-er Channel had filmed one of the cottages momentarily drifting in the tempestuous seas before a single wave exploded it into a thousand pieces of floating wood.

But by 2006 there were no empty lots, no evidence of loss, just a cluster of charming cottages only seconds from the ocean. A broker could be excused for not bringing up the past. The first time a new homeowner would hear about any kind of erosion was probably when a neighbor knocked on his door requesting that he cough up his $500,000 contribution to the community effort to pump offshore sand onto the beach, an operation that would have to be repeated every five to seven years. For without such renourishment, these cottages were but a single storm away from oblivion.

The history of Sconset is revealing. Any surfer who has spent time looking for a new surf break can tell you that the beach changes every year. During the 1830's ocean waves pounded directly at the toe of the bluff behind our cottage; our lot was still part of the seafloor. Then, as so often happens on a high-energy beach, the locus of erosion changed and a broad expanse of sand grew below the bank.

The first people to take advantage of the situation were commercial fishermen who built simple shacks on the beach and fished there all summer while their families enjoyed the more cosmopolitan pleasures of the town of Nantucket still wealthy from the whaling industry.

Then, around the turn of the century, a celebrated group of Broadway stars developed an artist's colony on the bluff. They hosted such luminaries as Rosalind Russell, Bette Davis, Truman Capote, and John Steinbeck. When Tallulah Bankhead was asked what she thought of New England society as she was being escorted off the island after an all night Sconset party she is reported to have yelled, "You can take Prout's Neck and shove it up Woods Hole."

Robert Benchley was the stalwart on the bluff. He had started the round table at New York's famous Algonquin Club, but on the island he was best known for soaking freshly caught bluefish in gin to sear off the smell of fish oil.

His son wrote a film about a Soviet submarine that threw the island into a tizzy after running aground on a Sconset bar, and his grandson wrote a film about a Great White Shark that throw the island into a tizzy after lunching on several of its inhabitants. Come to think about it *The Russians are Coming, the Russians are Coming* and *Jaws* are really just the same story with different antagonists.

The fun-loving "up-bank" artists spent every summer amusing themselves with tennis, musicals, and gambling in the Sconset Casino. Their servants, mostly black, settled into the former fishing shacks in the erosion-prone Codfish Park. Today a few of the "down-bank" cottages are still owned by the original black families, the rest by wealthy white summer folk.

Today the main topic of conversation on Sconset continues to be erosion. The 100-foot high cliffs still look out over the Atlantic Ocean and honeybees still sip sweet nectar out of the twenty-foot high privet hedges that hide the five million dollar homes on Baxter Road. The road used to lead to the Sankaty Head lighthouse. But the lighthouse is no longer there. It was moved off the rapidly eroding cliff in 2007. In fact, seven of the Baxter Road homes have been moved from the ocean side of the street to the inland side of the street which is now only 29 feet from the edge of the cliff.

The net worth of this single street is greater than several small Latin American countries combined. One homeowner sold his family owned cable TV system for close to $7 billion dollars. He could certainly afford his portion of the proposed $25 million dollar revetment designed to slow the erosion of the clay filled Sconset cliffs.

The homeowners had tried several systems before, including bluff terracing, an expensive dewatering system and Geotubes. But they had all failed spectacularly leaving adjacent beaches covered with tons of terracing boards, pipes and unsightly Geotube material. Town meeting had responded by passing a moratorium on building any further anti-erosion devices until the completion of a comprehensive beach management plan or the end of August 2013 whichever came first.

But the winter storms of 2112-2013 changed the dynamics of the situation. Thirty feet of the top of the cliff had cascaded into the Atlantic Ocean and now most of the multi-million dollar homes and the street with its water and sewer lines were only 29 feet from the edge. You didn't need to be a rocket scientist to figure out the math. Another winter like the last one would see several hundred million dollars worth of homes and infrastructure cascading down into the Atlantic Ocean.

The Sconset Beach Preservation Fund responded by pushing for the $25 million dollar project to build an 18-foot high rock revetment designed to withstand a hundred year storm and a two-foot rise in sea level. The name of the homeowners' organization was ironic. Like Galveston's 1900 seawall built to almost the same dimensions, the Sconset revetment would cause the public beach to wash away eventually leaving homeowners in nearby Codfish park in imminent danger.

But the board of selectmen were also cognizant that they stood to lose up to $300 million dollars in tax revenues and that they were legally bound to provide water, sewer lines and access to the 17 houses at the end of Baxter Road. Unlike on Plum Island, however, the local Conservation commission and several environmental groups were opposed to the expensive project.

The initial cost of building the revetment was going to be $25 million dollars. It would require ocean barges to park in the waves while excavators offloaded 3 to 5 ton interlocking boulders and placed them along the toe of bank. But then the homeowners would have to dump 2,000 truckloads of sand every year for 20 years on the ends of the revetment to prevent downstream scour. When all was said and done every homeowner would have to pay close to a million dollars to build and maintain the seawall.

John Merson, one of the Baxter Road homeowners who had moved his house back a 100 feet from the edge was more than happy with his new location even without the commanding ocean-front view. And was damned if he was going to pay so his recalci-trant neighbors could continue to enjoy their expensive views. At every public meeting, he kept asking the impertinent question, "At what point does it make more sense to relocate rather than keep paying for a rapidly eroding plot of ephemeral sand and clay?"

Sconset cliffs

Raising Caine

CHAPTER 35
HIGHLANDS, NEW JERSEY
August 9, 2013

August 9th broke cold, dark and rainy. I switched my computer on to the Salisbury Beach camera overlooking the deck of a surfside bar. Salisbury Beach and Plum Island were dark and desolate. You could see fencing around the former Sidewalk Café. In a few days the Massachusetts Department of Conservation and Recreation would tear down the long-abandoned eyesore and replace it with a natural new sand dune.

Bulldozers stood poised to raze a former go-cart track and amusement park to build 210 condominiums in the marsh behind the beach. The owners planned to dump 8 feet of fill into the marsh in order to prevent the condominiums from flooding. The site was behind the portion of the beach where waves from last winter's storms had almost drowned a woman in her living room, and destroyed over a dozen homes.

We had just entered the peak of the Atlantic hurricane season. There was a seventy percent chance that we would get 6 to 9 named storms and 3 to 5 of them were expected to be major hurricanes possibly as intense as Sandy or Katrina. Yet these projects were a barometer of just how determined oceanfront communities were to build up their waterfronts but how little they had done to prepare for the next storm.

On Plum Island people were hoping that repairing the Merrimack River jetty and building an artificial sand dune would save their homes from erosion, but these were dubious propositions at best. The same was true up and down the East Coast. Everyone had rushed out to prepare for the busy summer season, but few had done anything about the coming winter's storms.

Breezy Point was still several blocks of charred ruins in Queens, and 2,400 of her homes remained unoccupied. Nantucket was waiting to hear if the conservation commission would grant home-owners permission to armor Sconset Bluff and on Broad Beach mansion owners were waiting to see if the LA Department of Beaches would let them build their stone seawall.

The delays were indicators that our system of boards and regu-lations is not very good at responding to a rapidly changing envi-ronment. Homeowners, developers and environmental agencies would all benefit from a system that could respond more quickly to erosion and sea level rise. But, the Supreme Court had decided that property rights should trump sound environmental policy so it is almost impossible to arrive at any kind of coherent strategy to deal with rapid coastal change.

But Highlands New Jersey was proposing the most audacious plan of all. They had studied what Texas done after the 1900 Galveston Hurricane and were proposing that the Army Corps of Engineers spend $200 million dollars of taxpayers' money to ele-vate every house, flower and piece of grass in a community worth $574 million dollars.

They proposed to do this by moving everyone into shelters while their houses were put on pilings eleven feet above grade. Then the Corps would move in, build retaining walls, and dump million of tons of construction wastes behind the walls so that eventually the entire city would be raised eleven feet into the air.

The proposal wasn't scheduled to start until 2015, and construction could take at least three years. Meanwhile Highlands would have to endure at least 5 more years of potentially damaging storms.

But it seems like there is a more immediate solution. Route 36 runs through the town. Most of Highlands gets its name from what locals have always called the "dry" side of town that lies north of the street on land that rises to 266 feet and is the highest spot on the East Coast. But the town was built in the marsh on the "wet" side of Route 36; only 10 feet above mean high tide.

Highlands' town fathers could follow Nantucket's example and simply move the buildings to the other side of the street. But why do that if you can convince Congress to pay to elevate your town 11 feet into the air?

Then to add insult to injury the New Jersey legislature passed a bill that would allow people to construct buildings on piers that FEMA estimates would have a 26% chance of being flooded within the lifetime of their 30-year mortgages. This was not the way to plan for Sandy-like storms and sea level rise!

In comparison, Plum Island's proposal to build an artificial sand dune at homeowners expense was starting to look almost reasonable. But all these projects should have either been accepted or denied before August, and now it was getting late.

The Basin is where the mouth of the Merrimack River used to be.

PITA Photo Courtesy Mike Morris

CHAPTER 36
THE BASIN
August 17, 2013

August 17 was a perfect mid-summer's day. The sun flickered through row upon row of buttery green corn stalks as I drove from Ipswich toward Plum Island Sound. Their towering tassels of pollen and tufts of corn silk glowed in the early morning sun. These were signs that the cobs were now bulging with rich buttery kernels of sweet corn waiting to be paired with platters of clams and carafes of Pinot Grigio wine. Summer was at its very peak. You could not ask for a more perfect day.

When I arrived on Plum Island I took a left away from her statuesque homes overlooking the Atlantic. Another left led me to streets so narrow only one car could pass so I decided to park and explore by foot. I was immediately surrounded by brightly painted cottages with the same look and feel of any other island. I could have been on Codfish Park on Nantucket or Hope Town in the Bahamas.

I could hear snatches of conversation and the scraping of forks and knives on plates as people enjoyed their morning meals. But the neighboring bumblebees were already so drunk they could no longer fly. They had spent the last four hours sipping the sweet rich nectar of *Rosa Rugosa* bushes and were now so covered with pollen they could only stagger clumsily from blossom to blossom.

Two children were paddle boarding between boats being readied for fishing. I could hear the sharp cries of terns working over a small school of striped bass ahead of them. The bass were feeding on silverside minnows trying to hide in the shadows of the boats.

This marsh and beach rimmed body of water is called The Basin. In the 1830's this was where the Merrimack River flowed into the Atlantic Ocean. But fast flowing rivers are like garden hoses under pressure. They want to writhe back and forth like a watersnake swimming across a swimming pool.

Ever since the Ice ages the Merrimack had been able to writhe north or south creating new outlets to the ocean and building up new deltas of Paleolithic sand. I suspect that thousands of years ago the Merrimack flowed south behind Plum Island and joined with the Ipswich and Parker outflows debouching as one single river into the Atlantic Ocean off Crane's Beach. We don't know this for sure, but we do know that in the 1830's the Merrimack flowed down through the Basin to enter the ocean almost a quarter of a mile south of its present location. There it built up a delta that gradually helped force it to writhe north to its present location.

After this happened, longshore currents carrying sand north from the center of the island eventually closed the old exit to the ocean and built up the north side of the basin now called North Point to distinguish it from Old North Point with makes up the south side of the basin.

But Congress decided to stop all this foolishness in 1881 when it ordered the Army Corps of engineers to build a dike across the entrance of the basin and jetties to hold the river in one place. Today a geologist would look at this situation and say it is simply a matter of time before physics takes over and the mouth of the Merrimack switches again.

A similar situation exists three hundred miles northwest of New Orleans where the Army Corps of engineers has spent several billion dollars to prevent the Mississippi from flowing into the much younger and faster Atchafalaya River that flows impetuously south. Today the equivalent of seven Niagara Falls plunges over a sluice dam from the Mississippi into the Atchafalaya River, whose name takes about a half an hour to pronounce if said with a proper southern drawl.

A fortified tugboat patrols the area 24 hours a day to prevent 200-foot long barges from being swept into the maelstrom below. Geologists contend that the Corps is fighting a losing battle. During the 1973 floods engineers opened all the sluice gates and watched in horror as the roaring waters washed a massive guide dam down the river and the main dam vibrated so violently they feared it would collapse. Vibrations during an earlier flooding episode had ignited coal in a nearby railroad car. But such things seem so unlikely on a midsummers day in August.

Of course our situation is not nearly as dire as that on the Mississippi, but the jetties did have their own impact. As soon as they were built, they started to interfere with the longshore currents that had spent the last sixty odd years building up North Point. Many North Point homes were washed away and waves lapped the side of the Plum Island Lighthouse. Several cottages were moved off the outer beach to the protected waters of The Basin. But over time the jetties would settle and erosion would slow until the jetties were repaired again.

In a month the Corps is planning to finish repairing South Jetty. This will be the first time it has been repaired since 1970. Many have high hopes that this will save houses on Annapolis Way; others wonder what will happen to North Point.

CHAPTER 37
"GET YOUR GROINS OFF MY BEACH."
August 29, 2013

The August meeting of the Merrimack River Beach Association centered on preparing a letter to legislative leaders. It encouraged them to vote for money to repair the north side of the Merrimack River jetty system, even though representatives from the Army Corps of Engineers explained to the group that such decisions were no longer voted on by Congressional leaders. Past administrations had made the change to reduce the influence of pork barrel politics that used to be so prevalent in Army Corps of Engineers projects.

Toward the end of the meeting, a local marine engineer reported that towns only had until August 29th to apply for a state grant to repair or remove dams and seawalls. He suggested that building the proposed artificial sand dune might also be eligible for such funding.

But there was a much more obvious use for those funds. All the Plum Island houses lost to erosion had been just downstream of groins put in between 1962 and 1965. At the time people thought that groins were the way to go. But history had proved them wrong.

As we have seen, in 2008 three buildings including Jeannie's Restaurant and Gerri Buzzotta's house had been destroyed because they were immediately downstream of the Central Groin. Then, during last winter's March Northeaster, six more houses were swept away, three of them just downstream of the Fordham Way groin, and three more just downstream of the Annapolis Way groin.

"Get your groins off my beach."

The problem is that the groins interfere with the longshore currents that move sand north along this part of the beach. So, while the groins helped protect houses on their upstream side, they actually increased erosion on their downstream side with the tragic consequences we witnessed last winter.

The bill was designed to encourage communities to either repair or remove dams that block fish from swimming upstream to spawn and to repair or remove structures like seawalls that increase downstream erosion and make beaches steeper and more dangerous for swimming.

It is clear that the intention of the bill was to encourage the removal of dams but that language about repairing seawalls had been added to make the bill more palatable to the more recalcitrant members of the legislature. But the essence of the bill remained, $10 Million dollars were available to repair or remove dams and $10 Million dollars were available to repair seawalls. If legislators could convince the state to look the other way when the seawalls had been built on Plum Island, surely they could convince the state to remove groins that were exacerbating the problem.

If any community were eligible for these funds it was would surely be the town of Newbury. Nine of her houses had been lost and 43 had been declared uninhabitable because of the three groins.

It might be easy to convince the state to provide money to remove the groins, but it would be difficult to convince the town to apply for the money. Most of Newbury's board of selectmen and most of the members of her conservation commission were skeptical of the Wetlands Protection Act even though they were sworn to uphold its regulations. Plus it would be difficult to convince homeowners that removing such so-called anti-erosion devices would actually protect their homes. It just seemed too counterintuitive.

But the evidence was surely there. Perhaps the best strategy was not to go to the conservation commission or the board of selectmen but to appeal directly to the common sense of Newbury voters. They could request that town officials apply for funds to remove the groins. But you would need to have an organization push to have the item included on the warrant for the next town meeting.

But it was also clear that it would be counterproductive for such an organization to make any outrageous claims. You could not give any guarantees that removing the groins would save the houses indefinitely, that would all depend on the strength and frequency of future storms. But you could say with some degree of confidence that removing the groins would slow the rate of erosion and give homeowners a few more precious years in their homes, as well as bringing back the wide, safe beach that everybody remembered from their childhood days.

The wide beaches we remember from our childhood days, Plum Island, 2013.

CHAPTER 38
"WHY THAT'S UNCONSTITUTIONAL!"
2013

On August 22 I returned to Plum Island to look at the condition of the beach as we approached the peak of the hurricane season calculated to fall on September 10th. The beach was already steeper and more dangerous than it had been last summer. Occasional pieces of construction material still floated in the waves and cluttered the ocean floor. The problem would only get worse as winter storms removed sand from on top of the sharp stone seawalls and waves scoured away the beach downstream and in front of the offending structure.

A rusty scaffolding of angular pilings jutted from the top of the narrow duneline. Apparently the Buzzotta family had abandoned their plans to rebuild their mother's house on the almost the same footprint as before.

Tom Gorenflo had just finished framing the new house he was building on Southern Boulevard and Milton Tzitzenikos was preparing to move his house onto pilings on the soundside of Annapolis Way. Bob Connors had shifted his infamous front staircase, which had dangled 40 feet above the beach all winter to the side of the house where it now provided him a second egress to escape future storms.

Other than that, there was little evidence that any of the 40 other homeowners who had sustained damage last winter had done anything to prepare for the fast approaching stormy season. Apparently nobody had been able to agree on who would pay for the artificial sand dune, and none of the federal grants had come through to relocate or elevate homes. It had been almost ten months after the storm that had started it all, hurricane Sandy.

But on the same day, the Province of Alberta announced that it would purchase all of the 250 Canadian homes that had been damaged by floods last summer. On June 20th easterly winds had started to blow warm humid air up the side of the eastern facing Rockies into a cold low-pressure area stalled over Calgary. This had caused almost 4 inches of rain to fall onto the normally arid area.

The rain had also melted the snow pack on the Front Range of the Rockies, which had further engorged the Bow and Elbow Rivers that flow through the city. The rivers had soon risen to three times their previous record, which had only been set in 2005.

In the span of less than three days the flow of the rivers had rocketed to ten times their normal rate. Four people had drowned and 100,000 had been evacuated.

Now, less than three months after the storm, the Province of Alberta was offering to buy out all of the 250 homes considered to be at greatest risk of being flooded again. The government planned to demolish the waterlogged houses to make way for public parks and open space designed to soak up overflow water in the event of future floods.

However, the Province of Alberta banned building future homes in the floodway zones, but said that if present homeowners wanted to remain they could only apply for one- time grants to rebuild their homes, after that they would be on their own. They would be ineligible for future disaster relief.

The provincial officials expected that the citizens of Calgary would accept the offer with the politeness so characteristic of Canadians, which only seems to disappear when the Boston Bruins are in town to play hockey.

If officials made the same offer in the United States they would be yelled off the stage. "How dare the government trample on people's rights to protect their homes? If I can buy a gun to protect myself, why can't I build a seawall to protect my home? The framers of the Constitution didn't give a good Goddamn about global warming, why should we?" And the curious thing about this argument is that the Supreme Court agrees.

Unlike Canada, the U.S. Constitution has the Fifth amendment which not only guarantees mobsters the right to remain silent but guarantees that a state cant prohibit people from living beside a flood prone river, on an eroding beach or in the path of a mudslide without just compensation—compensation which would drive states deep into debt.

The Supreme Court decided that such environmental regulations should be considered as illegal takings under the Fifth Amendment. It was an argument that would continue to reverberate around Plum Island as the winter approached.

High Sandy

Wooly Mammoth, Kristina Lindborg.

CHAPTER 39
THE HIGH SANDY PACHYDERM
August 31, 2013

A wicked bizarre New England story emerged on the last day
of August. Like so many New England stories, this one started in
New York. For the past sixty years Federal agencies including the
Army Chemical Corps and Homeland Security had been studying
animal diseases on a pork chop shaped piece of land off the outermost end of Long Island. It went by the innocuous name of the
Plum Island Animal Research Facility.

But in 2008, Congress voted to relocate this bioterrorism
laboratory to a place called of all things; Manhattan, Kansas, and
to sell the island to be developed. But who would want to live on
an island riddled with Anthrax and Rinderpest spores? First the
government had to conduct an exhaustive study to see whether
the research had left behind any contamination.

During the course of the study, an environmental group found
an old newspaper article about the discovery of the remains of a
woolly mammoth on the island in 1879. They were elated because
it meant that more archaeological studies would have to be done
before the island could be sold.

The New York media ran with the story, but it never quite rang
true. The article said the massive skull; backbone and leg had
been discovered near a life saving station. But there had never
been a life saving station on Plum Island in New York!

Eventually a librarian discovered that the article had originally
appeared in the old Newburyport Herald and was about Plum
Island Massachusetts, not Plum Island, New York. A local Long

Island paper had lifted the article word for word, as was their wont in those days, saying, "the skull was between two and three feet wide and there was a length of backbone over seven feet long. In form the skull was like that of an elephant and the leg bone as of enormous solidity when it belonged to the animal buried there."

Once the story shifted back to New England more questions emerged. Exactly where had the bones been found? Where were they now, and what significance did they have for modern day Plum Island?

The article said that "gentlemen" had found the skeleton protruding from, "an elevation of sand know as 'Brothers' Beach,' 150 feet long and 50 feet high, one of the largest sand hills on the island. Latterly the winds have blown it away, so that the sand dune has lowered to a height of only a few feet."

The problem was nobody knew where Brothers Beach had once been. Jerry Klima, a former selectman from Salisbury who had studied numerous historic maps of the island thought that it was probably one of the places where people congregated after the Civil war to enjoy their weekend picnics.

But the original article had also said that the site was near a life saving station. In 1879 there was only one life saving station on Plum Island and it was in the center of the island in a place now known as High Sandy. Today High Sandy is located in the Parker River Wildlife Refuge between parking lot 1 and 2. I drove down there to investigate but finally gave up. The original site was now probably under ten feet of water and a hundred feet offshore.

The other mystery was where the bones are now. I called up all the usual suspects; the Peabody Essex Museum in Salem, the Peabody Museum at the Andover Academy in Andover, and what I still call the Museum of Comparative Zoology at Harvard. The curator of vertebrae and invertebrate Paleontology Jessica Cundiff checked through her Harvard database and found nothing. She suggested that if the bones were ever found they would make a stunning exhibit in the Parker River Wildlife Refuge's new auditorium near the entrance to the island.

The article had also mentioned that the bones were already crumbly from being interned so long in the drying sands of the sand dune. We agreed that the remains of the bones were probably crumbling away in the attic of one of the old sea captain's houses on High Street.

Perhaps the most significant aspect of the bones was that they showed how much the dunes have migrated and the beach has eroded since 1879, to say nothing of since the end of the last Ice age. There is even the possibility that this pachyderm died in the wake of a comet impact in Quebec that wiped out most of the North American mega-fauna 12,900 years ago. This caused local Paleo-Indians to switch from being big game hunters to small game hunters and gatherers which eventually led to agriculture.

But in 1879 the beach was close to two hundred feet east of its present location and the winds were still pushing sand dunes over the old Paleolithic drumlins. The beach was still eroding back at the rate of two to three feet a year. When will another woolly mammoth emerge from the center of Plum Island? Only time will tell...

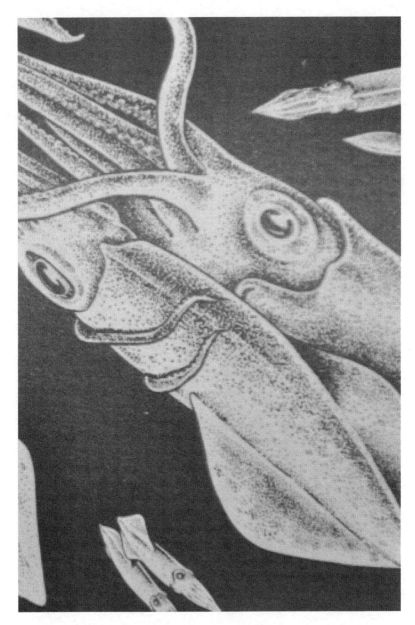

Mating squid. Robert Jon Golder

CHAPTER 40
AT AN ANCIENT ORGY
September 5, 2013

In early September I decided to visit the Parker River Wildlife Refuge to see where the woolly mammoth had been discovered. But, instead of finding evidence of geological change, I found evidence of biological change in all its teeming fecundity.

The early morning sun glistened off gelatinous masses of squid eggs stranded in sandy tidal pools. Last night the quivering rays of the full moon filtered through writhing multitudes of these fleshy, foot-long mollusks. They were congregating on the ocean floor to mate and lay their eggs.

Males darted through the school trying to herd individual females away from the pack. Some of the females seemed to be more in demand than others, and the males had to grapple, struggle and occasionally bite their opponents in order to secure an unattached female.

Eventually one of the males would separate a female from the group and the two would swim entwined in each other's tentacles while the male held his median arm aloft in an elegant "S" shaped courting curve. Chromatophores flared up and down the male's body and an intense reddish- brown spot pulsated between his eyes. When another male approached the spot would intensify and dark splotches would appear along the side of his body nearest the challenging male.

Then the male glided below the female and attempted to grasp her around the middle. She pushed his arms away and darted aside. Again they swam side by side through the frenzied squid.

He tried again. This time she did not resist. His arms moved forward toward her mantle opening.

Holding her in his eight strong distal tentacles he used one of his long median tentacles to reach into his own mantle and withdrew a bundle of spermatophores from the tip of his muscular penis. Then, with one quick motion he plunged the spermato-phores bundle deep into her mantle where it ejaculated splattering reservoirs of sperm onto the walls of her oviduct.

Within five to ten seconds their mating was over and the female turned her attention to spawning. She reached into her mantle and withdrew an egg capsule encased within a thick mass of sperm impregnated jelly. Holding the capsule before her she swam toward the bottom ignoring the advances of her still amo-rous mate.

Finally she located a fucus-covered rock and plunged into the fronds of the leafy brown algae. Then with a series of twists and turns she entwined the egg capsule into the fronds and flushed the eggs one more time with her siphon before darting back to her suitor.

Contact with the seawater hardened the egg jelly and the sight of the new egg mass elicited renewed frenzy among the other cephalopods. One by one other females mated and swam to de-posit their egg capsules until a mass of six-inch long egg capsules lifted gently toward the surface to confound this early morning beach walker.

All night long thousands of predatory fish that had also cruised through the school gorging themselves on the succulent squid bodies. But by dawn those squid who had made it through the night had died of sheer exhaustion. Millions of their pale white bodies littered the ocean floor amidst the opalescent masses of eggs that would produce next year's generation of squid.

There must have been some human fishing going on as well. I counted three undersized striped bass on the shore. They had to have been hooked and released during last night's feeding frenzy.

But this is a new ritual on this beach. 2012 was the first year that large numbers of squid started to swim north of Cape Cod to spawn. Global warming has finally warmed the oceans enough to cause such rapid biological changes.

Building a 200 unit apartment building in the middle of a marsh.

CHAPTER 41
THE KARTLAND ARMS
September 9, 2013

On September 9th Salisbury Massachusetts signed off on one
of the dumbest post-Sandy schemes on the East Coast. Beach
Realty a shadowy firm with a New Hampshire address wanted to
build a 200 unit apartment complex in the middle of a marsh that
floods at every high tide. One wonders what the young couples
living in the one and two bedroom apartments would do in the
middle of the summer when the swimming pool was surrounded
by greenhead flies, to say nothing of the winter when the National
Guard had cut off their access to the mainland and the complex
was surrounded by sea water.

But I guess the New Hampshire developer knew all about building coastal homes in an era of rapid sea level rise. New Hampshire has eighteen miles of coast to worry about -- Massachusetts
has fifteen hundred.

According to the local paper the developer would use "3,000
trucks carrying 20 to 30 cubic yards of fill and drive through
Salisbury every six minutes for 30 to 40 days," to build the artifi-i
cial island. Then he would construct a series of detention ponds
to prevent sheets of untreated storm water from flooding into the
marsh the way it did when the site housed a miniature golf course
and a go-cart track.

Unlike Highlands New Jersey that wants to raise their existing
community 11 feet or Galveston that raised their existing city 27
feet, there are no structures on this site except the remains of a
giant plastic whale that used to adorn the miniature golf course.

Salisbury certainly needs affordable housing but why build an apartment complex with a pool and a clubhouse in the middle of a bug-infested marsh? Why not build the town's largest new development on nice firm bedrock in an upland area?

Perhaps the $10,000 permitting fee paid just to get permission to dump fill on the site helped explain the lure of the project. That, plus Salisbury's third auction in seven years of properties with unpaid taxes. Many of the properties had a history of wetlands related issues and were subject to Department of Environmental Protection approval, others could help abutting owners whose lots were presently so small they were illegal.

In the words of the town's chief assessor, "Sportsmen might find a couple of the marsh lots interesting recreational opportunities. They have access to the Merrimack River and would be perfect acquisitions for hunters, fishermen and canoe or kayak enthusiasts. Prices for such wetland lots would be a modest amount, starting with bids at $2,500."

The auction reflected the fact that Salisbury, was also a cash-strapped town with thousands of acres of marsh, far better for kayaking or canoeing than housing suburban style apartment complexes.

The Salisbury conservation agent, Michele Rowden did not seem entirely comfortable with the Conservation Commission's decision to go ahead with the Kartland project, but her hands were tied. During the 1970's and 1980's she could have turned down such a foolhardy project because of environmental or safety concerns.

But because the conservative leaning 1992 Supreme Court had determined that any environmental regulation that decreased the value of a developer's property should be considered a "taking" Salisbury would have to reimburse the New Hampshire developer the $2.5 Million dollars he paid for the 13-acre lot. In essence, Michele's hands were tied.

Hopefully the next time Salisbury auctions off a lot better suited for canoeing than housing an apartment complex, either an environmental group or a governmental agency will have enough money to purchase the lot.

Approaching Storm

CHAPTER 42
SEASIDE HEIGHTS
September 12, 2013

Bill Akers couldn't believe his eyes. The $8 Million dollar board-walk he had worked so hard to rebuild after Hurricane Sandy was in shambles. A massive fire had ripped through the structure on September 12th destroying fifty small businesses. "Oh my God," thought the mayor, "The contractors were probably so rushed they fouled up the wiring."

But investigators from the Bureau of Alcohol, Tobacco Firearms and Explosives ruled that the fire had started under a frozen custard shop whose wiring had been done in the 1970's. However sand washing over the boardwalk during Hurricane Sandy had abraded the plastic coating off the wires allowing them to be exposed to the salt water.

Ocean County Prosecutor Joseph Coronato concluded that the wiring had been inaccessible to the public, "We will never really know why the wires came in contact with each other." Local authorities had even pulled the financial records of all the businesses involved to make sure that nobody had any financial reason to start the fire. "We left no stone unturned. This was not a suspicious fire." Gnawing rats are usually blamed in such instances.

But Angela Papoutakis worried about the findings. She knew that salt crystals and humidity could short out an electrical system, long after a storm had passed. Her electrician had re-inspected all their wiring and the sprinkler system in her pizzeria after the storm and she wondered out loud if the town had inspected the other properties as adequately.

Whatever the case, the boardwalk that Bill Akers had struggled so mightily to rebuild in time for the season had burned to the ground a week after Labor day. It did give one pause.

Now the beach was a mess. Fire officials had ripped out 25 five feet the new boardwalk and filled in the gaping hole with sand. They had essentially built a sand dune to stop the fire instead of the ocean. Governor Christie had stepped in to say that businesses affected by the fire could postpone filing their sales tax returns until October 21st and pledged that $15 Million dollars of the recovery money provided by the Federal government in the wake of Sandy would go to helping the businesses rebuild after the fire.

But even with Federal help it would be difficult for some businesses to survive both a hurricane then a fire, five months later. It would be a prelude to the problems Plum Islanders would face as they turned their attention to building their own artificial sand dune, even though we were already smack dab in the middle of the hurricane season. Hopefully they would have the sand dune finished in time for the coming winter's gales.

Inlet

CHAPTER 43
SANDY'S SILVER LINING
September 18, 2013

Mike Busch motored to the new inlet that Hurricane Sandy had carved out of Fire Island almost a year before. Now underwater beds of bright green photosynthesizing eelgrass swayed in the incoming tide and sea robins lay on the ocean floor eight feet below his boat. Mike loved what he saw. The bay was as clear as when he remembered it as a kid fishing in these same pellucid waters.

But that had not been the case for the past thirty years. Huge blossoms of brown algae had engulfed the bay every summer cutting visibility to only a few feet. The culprit had been the many houses and agricultural fields on Long Island. Tons of pesticides, lawn products and sewage had leached out of leaky septic tanks and washed off lawns and fields to over fertilize the waters of Great South Bay. The resulting brown tides had killed off almost all of the eelgrass and the shellfish beds that had once supplied half of all the clams consumed in the United States.

Eelgrass is the keystone species of this estuarine habitat. It is actually a higher plant, an angiosperm, similar to the flowers you might see in your garden. It has tiny blossoms that bloom in the spring and it releases its pollen directly into the salty waters.

Somewhere back in its early evolution this former land plant had moved back into shallow saltwater bays where it found no competition and thrived. Because of this strange quirk of evolution eelgrass has become what scientists call an indicator species because it must have clean clear waters so that enough sunlight can filter through the water column to allow its fronds to photosynthesis. But in the last thirty the brown tides had blocked out the sun causing most of the eelgrass beds to blanch and die.

But Hurricane Sandy had changed everything. It had burst through the barrier beach delivering millions of gallons of fresh clean salt water. Initially the new inlet was only a few feet deep and about forty feet wide. Thirteen men with shovels could have sealed it back up at low tide. But they didn't, and within a few months the inlet had grown to 1500 feet wide and over ten feet deep.

In the spring, fishermen had started seeing more fluke, seals and river herring in the bay. They hoped that the new inlet would help resurrect one of the East Coast's only populations of sea run brook trout. Even the clams caught in the Eastern part of the bay had nice big fat growth rings from gorging on all the plankton now rushing through the inlet on every incoming tide.

It would have cost millions of dollars for humans to have made these improvements, but nature had done it for free. However, there was a flip side to this new situation. Politicians had started to pressure the New York Department of Environmental Conservation to close the inlet because many of their constituents lived on the other side of the bay and feared that the break in the barrier beach would leave them susceptible to flooding. They pointed out that the Department had promulgated a breach contingency plan in 1996 that called for closing any inlets that did not fill in naturally.

But the break had been quietly building up its own constituency. It was already a popular destination. Boaters now enjoyed swimming and fishing on the shallow flats created by the new inlet and every weekend hundreds of people walked a mile out from Smith Point just to view the new phenomenon.

The Fire Island National Seashore had requested funds to study the inlet, but the Department of Environmental Conservation had already asked the Army Corps of Engineers for a plan to fill the inlet in.

But Nature had time on its side. The inlet had stabilized at 1500 feet. Now, instead of taking thirteen men with shovels to fill in the breach it would millions of dollars and an expensive government dredge to repair the damage.

The same thing had happened on Cape Cod's Pleasant Bay. An inlet had formed in April but by the time homeowners had a chance to put together a summer town meeting the price tag to fill in the inlet had risen to $4.1 million dollars. And on foggy nights the signs that homeowners had posted to read "Save our Shores" had somehow been altered to read "Save our Inlet".

So, on a sweltering night in late July, when the town moderator finally intoned, "All those in favor of the town's borrowing $4.1 Million dollars to fill in the inlet say aye," only two defiant voices answered in the positive.

"Those opposed?"

Six hundred "No's" roared back like a wave of rolling thunder.

Now I know that New Yorkers are known more for their chutz-pah than their wisdom. But one can only hope that in this one small instance they will follow the lead of their neighbors to the north. Of course they never have before.

Ocean waves washing toward the sewer lines on Fordham Way

CHAPTER 44
PLUM ISLAND
October 10, 2013

Strands of the Plum Island story started to unravel in early autumn. On September 30th Newburyport City Councilor Richard Sullivan proposed that the Council release details of a closed-door session it had held about the Plum Island water and sewer system.

The water and sewer system was the reason that so many houses had been remodeled into year round dwellings. But the system had lost pressure on several occasions stranding the homeowners without water or sewer services. Several of the water mains were under the streets that had eroded during the winter storms and nobody knew if the system had failed because of the storms, faulty construction, or both.

The city was trying to decide whether to sue Camp Dresser McKee the engineering firm that had done the work, and didn't want to tip its hand. But Councilor Sullivan was running for mayor and was not above making a bit of political hay.

Mayor Donna Holaday and Allison Heartquest, the councilor who represented Plum Island opposed the measure, but it put all of the politicians in a tight spot. Another councilor who was also running for mayor suggested that the measure be sent to committee but he was shot down with little fanfare.

By the end of the night, 5 Councilors voted for the proposal and only three had voted against it, but two had voted present and one was absent because of a death in the family. This odd configuration of votes had killed the measure because it had failed to receive a clear majority.

But the vote was really just a sideshow. The main event had started several weeks before when Marc Sarkady sent an urgent e-mail to his Plum Island neighbors. The President of the Plum Island Foundation had decided to postpone the foundation's annual $100 a plate fund raiser so that he could devote his full attention to the Foundation's beach mining proposal.

Marc had recently spoken to his local engineer, who had come up with a reasonable path to move the project forward. But it would require that all the primary dune homeowners south of the Center Groin had to buy into mining the beach in order to build an artificial sand dune. Marc knew it would be an uphill fight.

Last winter's beach scrapping project had left a bitter taste in many people's mouths. Six homeowners had lost their homes and had not fully committed to rebuilding them. Why should they spend $6,000 to protect their empty lots?

Almost thirty people had spent close to $40,000 a piece to build illegal seawalls that would only increase the rate of erosion because they had been built without backing material. The seawalls would just accelerate the energy of the waves flowing between the rocks causing them to scour sand out from behind the seawall faster. Why should they pay $6000 for sand to protect their rocks?

But, if these homeowners did not sign on to the project there would be gaping holes and the sand dune would not hold. However, the town, the state, and the Army Corps of Engineers had all agreed that they would permit the sand dune if the homeowners committed to the project within a week!

Four homeowners had already paid $4,000 to do the initial work and Marc and the foundation agreed to pay $3,000 to complete the design. But neither he nor the foundation could afford to cover additional costs, therefore they needed signatures and an initial $3,000 from every homeowner to proceed.

In the end Marc was only able to convince 7 people to commit to the project. At the October 4th meeting of the Merrimack River Beach Users Association he admitted defeat but gamely suggested he would try again in the Spring when waves would have more time to compact the sand, but that left nobody with protection for the winter ahead.

None of the homeowners had received federal grants to elevate or relocate. Milton Tzitzenikos had used his own money to move his house across Annapolis Way and another homeowner had demolished his former cottage and hired Tom Gorenflo to build a new permanent home less than a hundred feet from the edge of the dunes.

People were back in most of the thirty-nine houses that had been condemned in March, but none of the homeowners had done anything substantial to protect their homes. It was not a good way to head into the winter storm season.

On top of that, Marc had received of an unwanted surprise. When he opened his bill from the Federal Flood Insurance Program's agency he discovered that his premium had increased from $3,500 a year to $25,000 a year, an increase of almost 900%. It was not a good Halloween present.

Flood Insurance?

CHAPTER 45
FLOOD INSURANCE?
BUILD AN ARK!
October 1, 2013

Jonathan Rausch felt terrible. He had just told the owners of a nine unit condo on Hollywood Beach that their new flood insurance policy was going to cost them $36,584, seven times more the $5,126 he had quoted three weeks before.

The owners were freaking out. The new rates made their Florida condos unsalable. Who could afford to pay $36,000 a year for insurance on a condo only worth $360,000?

People all over Florida were feeling the same sticker shock. They hadn't been able to buy flood insurance from private companies for years. The companies had all pulled out of the Florida market after Hurricane Andrew. The same was true in other hot spots like Cape Cod and the Outer Banks.

In those places, homeowners could only purchase flood insurance through the Federal Flood Insurance Program. More than a third of all the program's policies were on Florida homes and their rates were rising faster than the space shuttle departing Cape Canaveral.

The problem started in 1965 when Hurricane Betsy destroyed large swaths of Florida causes $1.4 Billion dollars in damages making it the most costly hurricane at the time. Legislators decided it made more sense to provide cheap insurance rates to homeowners rather than for the government to keep paying for disaster relief so they established the Federal Flood Insurance Program.

But not enough homeowners ever signed up for the program to cover the costs of paying for major storms, so the government had been forced to subsidize the policies. The program had fallen $18 billion dollars into debt after Katrina and $24 billion dollars after Hurricane Sandy. That had prompted Congress to pass the 2012 Biggert-Waters bill, which was designed to raise the rates for federal flood insurance until they reached market levels.

But nobody paid very much attention when rates went up on secondary homes at the start of 2013. It was hard to feel very sorry for millionaires losing subsidies on their beachfront homes. It was like forcing the 99% percent who lived on the bottom of the economic pile to subsidize the lifestyles of the 1% percent who lived on the top. However, a study done in 2010 had shown that without raising the rates it would take over a hundred years without a major storm for the National Flood Insurance to recoup it's losses -- and that was before Hurricane Sandy in 2012, and Hurricane Irene in 2011!

However, the changes were also aimed at the 1.1 million owners of small businesses and primary homes that were also being subsidized as well. Their rates had started to kick in on October 1st when owners of primary residences who had made repetitive claims for flooding losses saw their rates rise 25% -- and would continue to do so every year until the rates reached market value.

The situation was compounded by the fact that FEMA had released new flood maps that had put many people in more expensive flood zones, generating "Stop FEMA days" in coastal communities up and down the coast.

On Cape Cod, Rick Bashian who lived beside Pilgrim Lake in Truro challenged the government to produce evidence that waves had crossed his street in the past hundred years. But Truro's board of selectmen refused to enter the fray on his behalf, claiming that they were not scientists and didn't have the expertise.

Deborah McCutcheon of the conservation commission agreed, "A lot of very careful scientific data and measuring went into that analysis." But the entire Massachusetts Congressional delegation had already sent a letter to their leadership requesting that money be given to the National Academy of Sciences to double check the science before they would allow the changes to go into effect. U-Mass oceanographer Brian Howes discovered that FEMA's contractors had used wave data from the steep West Coast to make maps along the East Coast that has a much flatter coastal plain.

But time was running out. Homeowners only had until October 17th to appeal the inclusion of their properties in the new flood zones. Barring any changes, insurance rates based on the new maps were scheduled to go into effect in June and nobody knew if any allowances would be made because the Federal government had been shut down for two weeks! It was about the time that Noah would have started building his ark.

Build an Ark!

Erosion cuts toward the sewer line. The house is on the other side of the sewer line below Annapolis Way.

CHAPTER 46
SEWER TALK
October 16, 2013

On October 16th Donna Holaday finally had a chance to talk about her sewer issues. It was in front of a standing room only crowd at PITA Hall. Bob Connors exhorted people to stay on topic as the Newburyport mayor expressed her disappointment with Camp Dresser & McKee. "This is totally unacceptable, totally unacceptable what they have done."

Donna had not been able to speak about the issue for several months. The state's attorney general office had requested that she sign a gag order not to discuss the issue until the completed a criminal investigation of the construction of the project.

City inspectors had discovered corrosion in the system that they believed could lead to the failure of the islands 187 water hydrants as well as leaving up to 750 homes without sewer and water services. The main water line had burst near the Plum Island bridge in 2011 and again during hurricane Sandy in 2012.

The city had found out that about the weaknesses in the system after a car smashed into a water hydrant in February and they had been so concerned about the amount of corrosion they had canceled the annual flushing of the pipes for fear that it might cause further damage.

Senator Tarr closed the meeting by counseling residents to remain patient as the state decided whether to sue or settle out of court.

Mike Morris and Rob Thieler

CHAPTER 47
MIKE MORRIS
October 21, 2013

Mike Morris was nervous. The head of the new Storm Surge group had to introduce the first speaker of their fall lecture series and nobody was sure how many people would show up. For the past two weeks the group had been trying to decide whether to hold the meeting at the Parker River Wildlife Refuge or the Newburyport Library because of the government shutdown.

But at the very last minute the audience surged through the doors and admired the exhibits and well-appointed auditorium. The talk was on steps that could be taken to curb global warming but the speaker was from Canada so he was too polite to mention that the AC was going full blast and all that carbon dioxide was going into the atmosphere and would remain there for over a hundred years raising sea levels in places like Plum Island.

Mike was the perfect person to head up the Storm Surge organization. His family had moved to the Newburyport area in 1973 and he started surfing when he was twelve.

"I was always the kid you saw riding his bike to Plum Island holding my surfboard under my arm."

In high school Mike found a window on the top floor of the school building where he could look out at the mouth of the Merrimack River to see how the surf was running. He was always the first of his friends to shoot out the door and find the best surf break.

At U-Mass Amherst he took all the courses he could find in marine biology and oceanography so he could understand wave sets and beach dynamics. After finishing college he started a BMW repair shop in town and called it Schneller motors in homage to his German mother. But "Schneller" didn't stand for anyone's name. It meant faster in German.

Mike used what he had learned in college when he and his wife Jennifer bought a cottage on Plum Island. He knew not to buy near the marsh because that was where the worst flooding would occur during storms.

He also remembered that you should look for an old growth forest if you were going to buy a house on a barrier beach. The old trees signaled that the area hadn't flooded for several decades. And of course he knew to find something well back from the crest of the barrier dunes.

Mike and Jennifer finally found the perfect cottage. It was in a copse of old trees half way down Harvard Way between the marsh and the dunes. But they elevated it eleven feet high on pilings just to be safe.

They were glad they had raised their house during the 2006 Mother's Day floods. Even with the pilings the water came to within a foot of the hot water heater on the first floor of their home.

After the storm everyone had different theories about how the beach had behaved. Jennifer had been elected as a selectman to the town of Newbury by then and after one of the interminably long meetings she came home and asked Mike to explain exactly how the beach really moved.

Mike used everything he had learned in college to explain as best he could but also became intrigued with the specifics of the Plum Island problem and decided to conduct his own photographic survey.

The first thing that didn't make sense is that everyone was saying that the sand flowed south down the beach. But if that was so, why did the sand collect on the downstream side of the groins to the south rather than on the upstream side to the north side where you would expect it?

Then he discovered some old charts made before the jetties had been installed and saw that the charts had arrows indicating where the currents flowed north. People were more aware of currents in the 1800's because they had to row against the currents to reach their fishing grounds off Plum Island.

Now Mike and Jennifer were trying to prepare for the future. They hoped they would be able to pay down the mortgage on both their homes on Plum Island and in West Newbury then sell them and buy something smaller. But it had become a sticky proposition. They had to visualize what would happen to both the island and the real estate market.

Mike felt they had one of the safest houses on the island but at some point somebody was going to own the last house on the island and he didn't want to be that person. His insurance rate was very reasonable but he wasn't sure if he could pass on those rates to a new buyer.

But he felt that he at least had a few years to make the decision. The hard part was seeing what his neighbors went through every winter. It was heart wrenching to watch his neighbors on lots where the dunes were migrating and where the island was trying to roll over.

He had watched it happen ever since he was a kid fishing for bluefish and tuna off his father's boat. They had always used an old utility pole behind the Sea Haven polio camp as their range. The camp had been built in the 60's and both the camp and its large circular pool used to be well behind the primary dune. Now the camp and pool were gone and the utility pole was sticking out of the beach. It would not be long before it too was washed away. It was unsettling to see how much the island had retreated in just his lifetime.

Flood maps

CHAPTER 48
FLOOD MAPS
October 25, 2013

Karen Lynch was beside herself. It had become almost impossible to sell homes on Plum Island, "We don't know what to tell people about what they will pay for flood insurance," declared the Newburyport real estate agent at the Merrimack River Beach Users Association's October meeting.

The problem was the Biggert – Waters bill that almost every member of Congress had voted for right after Hurricane Sandy. But now that their constituents were being affected the politicians were back peddling as fast as Lance Armstrong in front an anti-doping hearing.

Even the co-sponsor of the bill, Maxine Waters of California was frantically telling her constituents, "I certainly didn't intend for these types of outrageous premiums to occur to homeowners." Perhaps the Democratic Congresswoman just hadn't bothered to read her own bill. Her co-sponsor, the Republican Congresswoman Judy Biggert had lost her bid for re-election.

But Craig Fugate had read the bill. The highly regarded head of FEMA had replaced Michael Brown of "You're doing a great job Brownie," fame. Fugate told a Senate sub-committee in September that the Biggert-Waters Act didn't allow him any leeway to postpone the changes, just because they would make life difficult for coastal homeowners.

As a native Floridian, Fugate knew that that was really the point of the bill and exactly why it was so important. The same was true for the Massachusetts Congressional delegation. Almost every member of the delegation had voted for the Biggert-Waters bill.

But now that it was going into effect they were pushing to have the act delayed for three to five years, so "the science behind the creation of the new flood maps could be studied."

The purpose of the bill was to discourage people from buying and selling homes on places like Plum Island where houses had a history of tumbling into the ocean. For years coastal homeowners had been paying ridiculously low insurance rates then expecting taxpayers to pick up the tab so they could rebuild their homes on exactly the same footprint as before.

Fugate was correct. There was very little that FEMA could do to slow down the process. Homeowners had less than ninety days to hire an engineer to appeal the new FEMA maps that had put them in higher flood zones. Towns like Newbury that derived 40% of its tax revenues from its 800 residences on Plum Island had a lot to lose.

The head of the Newbury board of Selectmen, Joe Storey, pointed out that towns had to vote to accept the new maps at the end of the appeals process. If they didn't, nobody in the towns would be able to get Federal Flood insurance. That meant that banks had the right to foreclose on such properties. The same was true for the 400 Plum Island homes in Newburyport.

Senator Tarr tried to close the meeting on an upbeat note. He said he would go right back to his office and call FEMA so that someone could explain the contentious maps at the next MRBA meeting in November.

But the clock was ticking fast. The extremely mild hurricane season would be thankfully over, but the season for Northeasters was just beginning.

"Why would I want to live in a war zone?"

CHAPTER 49
"WHY WOULD I WANT TO LIVE IN A WAR ZONE?"
October 29, 2013

Mike Fromosky looked at the three-inch pile of complaints spilling out of his in-box. For the past few months the assistant administrator of Little Egg Harbor had been getting e-mails, phone calls, even old-fashioned letters from people complaining about their neighbors' homes—houses with holes in the roof, overgrown weeds, and the fetid odor of rotting slime mold emanating out of open doors and windows.

Mike had been trying to figure out how many of these houses had been abandoned, but it was tricky business. Four thousand Little Egg houses had been damaged by Hurricane Sandy and now homeowners were trying to figure out if their neighbors were still waiting for insurance money or if they had just walked away from their homes.

"But I'm like, how do I identify them? My house probably looked abandoned to my neighbors for about nine months," explained Fromosky to a visiting journalist.

Rebuilding had been slow, especially if people were still fighting for insurance checks or waiting to see if they were had been able to get government grants. And many of the houses in Little Egg Harbor didn't even qualify for government assistance because they had been second homes.

But the biggest problem was just coming into focus a year after the storm. How many people were going to lose their mortgages? Foreclosures had been on the rise in New Jersey even before Sandy but now they were 67% higher than they had been a year ago.

Only three people had moved back to one Little Egg Harbor street. But the thirty other homes on the dead-end street were surrounded with weeds and storm debris. Nobody had seen the owners since the Saturday before the storm.

Apparently some of the homeowners were still waiting for insurance money and the bank had taken over others. But the banks hadn't even torn down the moldy walls and removed the still soaking rugs from houses where small slimy mushrooms now proliferated. Just opening the front door of such a house was a startling nasal experience.

Further down the street, neighbors had collected a big pile of asbestos debris and left it on the curb. Hopefully the town would remove it before any more of the toxic asbestos particles leeched into the water system.

All this put Mike in a difficult position. The town had to start determining the condition of such houses and who actually owned them. Eventually he would have to obtain liens on the abandoned houses and pay to have them torn down.

But at the same time he was starting to get complaints that the town was harassing homeowners. He could understand that as well. The former victim knew just how long it could take to do all the paperwork and get financing to rebuild your damaged home.

Other towns were in the same boat. Over 16,000 New Jersey homeowners had canceled their insurance policies prior to Sandy and at least 100,000, and probably thousands more, owned second homes so they had been ineligible for Federal aid.

But all the owners were tapped out. Some were trying to slowly rebuild, others were trying to resell, but who wanted to buy a house that had just been damaged by a hurricane?

Thomas Kelaher, the Mayor of nearby Tom's River was also concerned that thousands of his homeowners had just walked away from their homes, "But they are under no obligation to tell us if they have abandoned their properties."

He had sent out surveys to determine exactly where the town stood in the rebuilding process. It was getting to the point where the town was going to have to do something. He realized that thousands of Tom's River homes had already turned into health hazards.

The situation made Mike Ehrenkranz feel fortunate that he had walked away from his Tom's River home. He had stopped paying for insurance once he had paid off his mortgage prior to Hurricane Sandy.

After the storm flooded his house with more than four feet of water he had sold his house and moved inland. "Now I'm cutting grass instead of raking stones, so my life is back in order."

"Of course I'm glad I moved out. My old neighborhood looks like a war zone. Why would I want to live in a war zone?"

Rob Thieler collecting garnet sand.

CHAPTER 50
IN THE BELLY OF THE BEAST
Plum Island November 4, 2013

On November 4th Rob Thieler made the long drive from Woods Hole to Plum Island Massachusetts. I had asked him to speak to our Newburyport Storm Surge group. Dr. Thieler was the perfect speaker, the kind of scientist who knew how to walk the walk, as well as talk the talk.

He had major grants to study beaches all over the world but he had also spent ten years helping his hometown plan for sea level rise. But I suspected that part of the reason he had accepted our invitation was that he also wanted to be in the belly of the beast.

Plum Island had become the bête noir of coastal geologists. Everyone had watched the islanders flaunt the law without repercussions. Rob wanted to see the condition of the illegal seawall that had been built up so haphazardly after last March's Northeaster.

After that storm Ken Kimmel had invited several prominent local geologists to attend a special meeting at the Department of Environmental Protection. Many of the scientists had helped craft the state's Wetlands Protection Law, which was widely regarded as one of best in the country. The state wanted to make doubly sure that they were interpreting the law correctly and making the correct long and short-term decisions in the emergency situation. As a government scientist, Rob had to be policy neutral but several of the other scientists had said what was on his mind anyway.

They all made the point that the kind of erosion that happened on Plum Island would keep cropping up and become worse in the coming decades. If the Department of Environmental Protection didn't enforce their own rules, then other communities would take it as a signal that as long as they "felt" they were in an emergency they could do whatever they wanted. They could also start using Plum Island as a precedent for future projects. It would be like the Wild West with Massachusetts having the same head in the sand posture as South Carolina.

Despite the meeting, the Department of Environmental Protection had not taken any action against any Plum Island homeowners who had powerful allies with deep pockets in the Pacific Legal Foundation. Apparently the state's legal counsel had warned Kimmel to back down.

But the DEP had an ace up its sleeve. It knew that both time and nature were on its side. Eventually the seawall would fall, more houses would be lost, and the seawall's sharp rock boulders would tumble onto the beach. Then the DEP could make the homeowners remove the boulders because they were a health hazard. It would be a bitter pill for homeowners. First they would lose their homes, then they would have to pay to remove their seawalls.

The stratagem probably wouldn't work. Plum Islanders had become used to flaunting the law. They might just ignore the fines and walk away from beach they had helped destroy. But it might send a message to other communities that they could be held accountable.

Plum Island was already being cited as a precedent in places like Nantucket where wealthy homeowners were trying to get permission to build their $24 Million dollar seawall that would wash away the island's beautiful Sconset Beach.

Rob finally met Mike Morris and I at the Plum Island Grille. We had planned it so Rob would arrive in time to see the island by daylight. As we approached the Central Groin Rob quipped, "It looks exactly like I remember it from Google earth." He had flown over the island several times in both large and small planes but this was the first time he would have a chance to see things up close.

He was not disappointed. The recent October high tides had scoured the beach. Waves had already washed away tons of sand leaving steep scarps that we had to clamber over in order to reach the houses. Purplish red garnet sand was everywhere. It showed that the autumn waves already had enough energy to winnow out the heavier sand and leave it just below several of the most vulnerable homes. It was not a good sign. It was only early November and the beach was already sporting its winter profile.

But the most ominous sign was the condition of the seawalls themselves. Most of the sand that homeowners had used to cover the seawalls had washed away. Now the sharp edges of the boulders were exposed and many of them had already tumbled off the seawalls and were lying in the sand.

If the beach already looked like this, what would it look like in the coming months? It did not bode well for winter.

Oysters

CHAPTER 51
INTRODUCING OYSTERS
November 11, 2013

In early November I donned my waders to scratch up some oysters. Mixed with mushrooms and chestnuts they would make the perfect stuffing for our annual Thanksgiving dinner. A seafood writer once described a raw oyster as nothing but a big fat gonad floating in a bath of seawater.

It is a fitting appellate for a mollusk that can produce a million eggs a summer and change sex several times during its adult life. And it is that fecundity that is also the key to our present interest in oysters.

I have watched this bed of oysters expand over the past ten years. When I arrived in Ipswich I was only able to find a few oysters in an isolated tide pool in the middle of the mud flats. They were protected because you had to walk across a hundred yards of boot sucking mud. A few years later I discovered another small patch on a small rock strewn island off Eagle Hill. Now the beds stretch for almost a mile up and down the estuary. It has been a rapid return to what these waters had been like during colonial times.

When the early discoverers explored America they were delighted to find that all her major estuaries were protected by ten-foot thick beds of oysters that were busy removing calcium and carbon dioxide out of the water to make their own form of natural concrete. The interlocking shells of the oysters were acting as breakwaters to protect East Coast harbors from storm surges and sea level rise -- to say nothing of providing inexpensive delicacies to anyone who bothered to walk out on the flats to harvest them.

They became the favorite seafood of both the rich and poor as they had been in Europe since Roman times. They were also the perfect seafood to ship because they could last for a month without refrigeration. Many a gold miner in San Francisco celebrated his new claim with a bushel of Ipswich oysters and several carafes of champagne.

But one of greatest environmental tragedies of all time occurred when America allowed her fishermen to deplete these East Coast beds and not return the empty shells. Immature oysters needed to be able to detect the scent of calcium carbonate coming off these shells so they would know to settle down and become sensible adult creatures.

That tragedy led to a simple form of aquaculture, though some Southerners might refer to it more as simply larceny. Fishermen from places like Cape Cod and Newburyport would sail down to the South, harvest young oysters then transplant them back into northern waters. After the oysters picked up the "terroir" of the local waters they would be marketed as Wellfleets, Cotuits or Eagle Hill oysters. It is not recorded whether this practice led to War Between the States but the war certainly stopped it.

In the wake of the recent spate of major storms cities are beginning to rediscover the role that oysters can play in cleansing our waters and protecting our shores from erosion. Each oyster can filter 40 gallons of seawater a day so the vast beds of colonial oysters used to keep the water crystal clear. Once the oyster beds were gone the fisheries and swaying beds of oxygen producing eelgrass disappeared as well.

But now many of these same cities are starting to reestablish oysters as living reefs to protect themselves from sea level rise. The Google foundation has provided money for cities like New York, Boston and New Orleans to start reintroducing oysters on their harbor floors and suspending them from floating aquacultural islands. They will soon have reefs of interlocking oysters built in far less time than it would take to build a concrete breakwater.

The city of Newburyport could do the same thing. For hundreds of years oysters were harvested from The Merrimack, Parker River and Plum Island Sound. But by 1861 most of the natural beds had been depleted however three families still shipped oysters from Norfolk and grew them out in the Parker River.

Today there is interest in reintroducing oysters in Plum Island Sound and along the vulnerable shores of Joppa Flats. It remains a relatively easy thing to do. The first thing you would have to do is figure out where oysters used to grow. Then would want to harden the bottom with old shells or suspend oyster bags from docks and rafts. The simplest thing would be to get permission to transplant a hundred adult oysters from another location like Eagle Hill, then stand back and watch what the natural fecundity of oysters can do.

Some people may be tempted to introduce the fancier Belon oyster from France. They tend to grow in siltier environments than our native Crassostrea Virginicus. But our beloved Virginicas hold the sweet taste of the Merrimack and Ipswich Rivers. Let the oyster snobs have mud oysters so redolent of zinc and umami. Let the French sniff that Virginicas are only good for unsophisticated American palettes.

On the Ipswich flats these mud oysters are reviled as the invasives they really are. In the 1950's a scientific scoundrel introduced some Belons into Boothbay Harbor, more escaped from our good friends at the Aquaculture Center in Salem. Now Belon are invading our native beds of oysters from Maine to Nahant. You might be tempted to impress a date with talk of belon, terroir and sophisticated palettes in one of Newburyport's fancy new oyster bars -- but I wouldn't recommend it on Eagle Hill.

A lot in the primary dune, Plum Island

CHAPTER 52
THE DEAL
November 26, 2013

Ralph Cox was having another deja vu. The defining experience of his life had been when the young UNH hockey player had
been cut from the 1980 Olympic hockey team – the miracle team
that had been immortalized on film and television.

He knew that the U.S. could only have 20 players but it had still
rankled to be the 21st player. And now he felt that it was happening all over again, with the house he wanted to build on Plum
Island.

In 1953 the Freemen of Plum Island gave 5.4 acres of land to
the town of Newbury to act as a buffer between the developed
part of Plum Island and the Parker River Wildlife Refuge. But by
2012, society was starting to realize that houses prevented barrier
beaches from moving naturally and communities up and down the
coast were deeding vulnerable land to adjacent parks.

The 5.4-acre lot was an obvious candidate to sell to the Parker
River Wildlife Refuge. Most of the land was unbuildable because
it was on wetlands or in shifting primary dunes. But there was one
buildable corner on a secondary dune and the town of Newbury
needed the money. For the second consecutive year voters had
turned down a tax hike that local officials considered to be critical
for Newbury's fiscal health, plus 40% of the town's tax revenue
already came from houses on Plum Island. It placed the small
community in a difficult conundrum.

Selectman Bear had described the lot as perhaps "the last big property on the East Coast," and the town put it on the market for $1.7 million dollars. But the original agreement stated that the town could only sell the land if town meeting passed the measure by a two-thirds vote. A neighbor, Scott Ackerley had added an amendment to the vote that stipulated that the town had to sell the land to the Refuge first, but the town did not offer a price the Refuge could afford, so the land went on the market again.

Several private buyers had looked at the property but none of them felt they could get permission to build on such a fragile area. But Ralph Cox was familiar with the permitting process and saw it as a simple matter of supply and demand. There were only a limited amount of oceanfront properties; demand was high so of course they were going to be expensive. Though he ended up only paying $550,000 for the purchase and sale agreement.

Cox had built his real estate career on developing waterfront property usually with Stephen Karp a billionaire real estate developer who Forbes had just added to their list of the 400 richest people in the United States.

Up until 2006, Cox had worked for Karp on a multi-million dollar project to develop Newburyport's low-lying waterfront as well as on Nantucket where Karp owned 75% of the island's downtown storefronts. He was controversial on the island because he hiked his rents on a regular basis, made his tenants adhere to strict regulations and was said to disregard the plight of long-standing businesses trying to cope with island's short selling season.

More recently Cox had gone into business on his own, building waterfront facilities in Boston and Seattle. The Boston lot was nicknamed Subaru Pier because it had been used to store automobiles just off the boat from Japan. Who was one of the former shareholders in the marine terminal project? Stephen Karp.

Apparently the Karp Cox business model was to make as much money as quickly as possible on waterfront property. It is obvious that Cox was not too concerned with the long-term consequences of sea level rise so he figured he had made a good deal on the Plum Island land.

But what he hadn't counted on were his neighbors and the DEP. In 2012 Sandy Lepore asked the state's Department of Environmental Protection to issue a superseding order on the Newbury Conservation Commission's permission to build.

The Newbury Conservation Commission had long been a nettle in the side of the state's DEP. Newbury was about the only town in the Commonwealth where the conservation agent was also the chairman of the commission and where the majority of commissioners were in the construction business. On almost any day you could see a bunch of developers laughing with the agent as he sat with his feet on the desk wearing his signature weekend stubble and tinted dark glasses.

Environmentalists felt intimidated by the setting. One former town employee described the scene around the agent's desk as being like a bunch of good ole Southern boys yucking it up with the county sheriff.

The Cox offer was contingent on getting permission from the DEP and the DEP was taking its time. They were still irked that the conscomm hadn't done anything to prevent the construction of the illegal seawalls and for rubber-stamping people's permits to rebuild houses on the primary dunes.

But this was a pretty straightforward case. The Wetlands Protection Act was clear, and it would be difficult to argue that not giving Cox permission to build would constitute a taking under the Fifth Amendment.

The wetlands act had already been in place when Cox made his offer. It was not like Lucas vs. the Coastal Commission of the state of South Carolina where the Supreme Court ruled that Lucas lost the value of his property because the state forbade him to build after he had bought his property.

It was clear that Society and the law were starting to grapple with the complexities of sea level rise. And Ralph Cox was starting to feel like he was going to be the last man to be cut from the team again. It was not a very good feeling.

.

Photos of erosion made it difficult to sell a house on Plum Island

CHAPTER 53
THE STIGMA
December 6, 2013

In December the Massachusetts Tax Appellate Board gave Plum Islanders an early Christmas present. Six people received tax breaks due to the "stigma" attached to homes on Plum Island because of photos of erosion that made it "difficult to sell ocean-front property on Plum Island despite depressed offering prices."

But the tax rolls also told another interesting story. Ever since the 1800's Plum Island had been dotted with inexpensive fishing shacks. But things had started to change. When the towns put in sewer and water lines and the national press started hyping the island as a steal for people looking for prime waterfront property.

The results were predictable. Summer shacks were torn down and replaced with year round statement homes. The Island saw its first million-dollar house in 2003 and just a few years later all the homes along Fordham Way totaled more than $25 Million dollars.

But everything started to fall apart when Gerri Buzzotta's house tumbled into the surf and the Army Corps of Engineers was called in to build a $12 million dollar sand dune to prevent the island from breaking in two.

Then in 2011 several residents of Northern Boulevard convinced the state to abate their taxes because of the "stigma" attached to photos of erosion on Plum Island. Now it was the turn of residents on Southern Boulevard, Fordham and Annapolis Ways.

Many people in town pointed out that it was the homeowners' fault. But was it really?

For the past 250 years, town, state and federal government agencies had been mismanaging this island. They built groins, jetties and allowed illegal seawalls. They buried faulty sewer and water lines in the shifting sands of the barrier beach and sold land in her primary dunes. They bent the rules so more people could hook into the water system than had been allowed. Then they encouraged homeowners to build on the lots to garnish a few more years of tax revenues.

It is not just the homeowner's fault. We are all to blame. Like Pogo in the Okeefenokee swamp, "We have met the enemy and he is us." However we are not alone. Almost every other coastal community has mismanaged their barrier beach islands as well.

So what do we do about it now? We have to roll up our sleeves and start to work with each other and nature to save these beautiful islands for homeowners and visitors alike.

A homeowner checks his land.

CHAPTER 54
DE SINTERKLAASTORM
December 6, 2013

On December 4th a North Atlantic low "bombed" over Iceland becoming extratropical cyclone Xaver with hurricane force winds. Xaver slammed into Scotland, England, the Netherlands, Germany and Scandinavia flooding major cities and ports.

It came in two days before the new moon, producing storm surges that were higher than those that killed over 2,000 people in the North Sea storm of 1953. In the Netherlands they nicknamed Xaver, De Sinterklaastorm because it arrived on their traditional St Nicholas day celebration.

England had to close the Thames Storm Surge Barrier through two tidal cycles in order to save its capital city and the Netherlands had to close all 62 locks of the Scheldt River Barrier system for the first time since 2007. But the difference between the English and the Dutch systems is instructive for Americans as we face more powerful storms.

England has put all her resources into the Thames Storm Surge Barrier. Without this single high tech solution, London after Xaver would have looked like New Orleans after Katrina.

But on the other side of the North Sea, the government of the Netherlands has started to take a different approach. The Netherlands has had more experience with floods than any other country. So much so, that the Dutch like to describe their country as a swampy marsh, full of stingy Calvinists who constantly remind foreigners that "God created the earth but the Dutch made the Netherlands." Our rejoinder of course, is that it was those same thrifty Dutch who traded Manhattan for Surinam.

But it is true that without its traditional system of dikes and windmills for draining water out of its polders, Holland would have long ago since retreated into Germany.

The Netherlands have several severe disadvantages. They are, after all "the lowlands," a marshy delta that drains several of Europe's largest rivers including the Meuse, the Rhine and the Scheldt. But 60% of Holland's GDP also comes from land that used to be underwater and Rotterdam, Europe's second largest city, lies 20 feet below sea level, like New Orleans.

The cadence of Dutch history is marked by floods; from 1170, the All Saints flood; to 1836, the Harlem Lake flood; to 1953, the North Sea Storm and the major river floods of the early 1990's and now the winter of 2013/2114.

The continual storms have claimed hundred of thousands of lives, but Holland's Calvinist spirit lives on, convincing the businesslike Dutch to continue spending their hard earned capital on improving their coastal defenses after every storm. The results have paid off. Holland continues to be the seventh largest trading country in the world and the Gateway to Europe.

The peak of the Netherlands hard engineering approach to shoring up her coasts occurred after the deadly 1953 North Sea storm. The Dutch immediately started investing over $40 Billion dollars to build a series of dikes designed to protect the entire length of the coast. This Delta Works program included the Rotterdam Barrier that was longer than the Eiffel Tower lying on her side. The barrier can be closed during a storm, but opened quickly afterwards so that Dutch businessmen wont lose any trade to competing ports in Germany, Belgium and Denmark.

But after the 1990's river floods, the Dutch realized that they needed another approach. If they wanted to continue living in their country, they would have to learn not to just fight Mother Nature but to control human behavior as well. This meant they would have to move people out of the dangerous floodplains to make room for wider rivers. They called this new mindset "Leben med water."

In the countryside, the Netherlands have spent $3.1 billion dollars to move levees back and make their rivers wider. In Rotterdam they have designed underground parking lots and skate parks that can store water during times of flood, and in rural areas they have removed dikes and levees so water can purposefully flood back into natural floodplains that had disappeared from the landscape for over two hundred years.

But the government also created new land and housing on protected mounds in the floodplains so farmers could still be close to their original family owned farmlands. It was not an easy solution but it protected hundreds of thousands of people in downstream towns, villages and cities.

But it is the Dutch Sand Engine that holds the greatest promise for America's barrier beach communities. As part of their "Building with Nature" program, the Dutch pumped 21 million cubic meters of sand onto a natural sand reservoir area of the coast where waves and wind, nature's sand engine, would move it naturally downstream to build up dunes and beaches. This $70 Million dollar project will make sand renourishment unnecessary for the next twenty years saving several million dollars.

The same thing could work on Plum Island but you would have to change the Army Corps of Engineers regulations and remove the groin field that blocks sand from flowing naturally to the developed part of the island.

When the Army Corps renourishes a beach now, they are required to do it in the cheapest possible way. On Plum Island, this means they can only pump sand out of the Merrimack river and dump it on the other side of the south jetty, instead of pumping it to the center of the island where it would naturally flow downstream to widen and protect the beach.

If the Army Corps could alter this one small rule they would also be able to protect the developed part of Plum Island for perhaps a decade without further renourishment. Then Plum Island could return to being one of the safest and most beautiful beaches on the East Coast.

Here, the new seawall has already slumped exposing two houses to being under-mined by ocean waves.

CHAPTER 55
THE SEAWALL
December 15, 2013

In mid-December I had some time to kill before attending a
Christmas play in Newburyport, so I decided to see if the December 15th storm had done any damage to Plum Island. When I
walked out onto the beach I couldn't believe my eyes.

Three houses were damaged and teetering on the edge; waves
had washed into Harry Trout's yard from across the street where
he had lost his first house last March. That meant that the ocean
had been flowing over the sewer lines buried under Fordham Way.

But the most ominous feature on the beach was the state of the
"emergency" seawall. Now it stood fully exposed in all its massive
glory. We had never been allowed to see its full bulk before. The
town of Newbury had closed the beach during the seawall's hasty
construction. Then the homeowners had quickly covered the wall
with tons of sand before the beach reopened.

However, it was now easy to see that the seawall had been
simply thrown together. Several half-ton boulders had already
tumbled off its 40-foot high face and the wall of five-ton concrete
blocks that had been built in the 1970's had collapsed and was
now lying on its side on what was left of the narrow beach.

I had to clamber over a rock field of slippery loose boulders to
get to the other side of the groins. Someone had written, "Stay Off,
Loose Rocks," on the face of the seawall. I suppose it was meant
to be a warning for any beach goer with litigious ambitions.

But the main problem with the seawall was that nobody had laid down any erosion fabric behind the seawall so now waves crashing through chinks in the boulder seawall increased their speed so they had more energy to undermine the wall. You could already see signs of this happening. Soil in the lots above the seawall had already started to slump exposing deep fissures in the bank. The fissures would have to be cordoned off with police tape so nobody would fall into the chasms forming between the shifting boulders.

The most frightening aspect of all this damage is that it had not been caused by a major storm. I had spent the morning monitoring beach cameras up and down the coast and conditions had not been that severe. The winds had only been blowing at 35 knots, the tides had been moderate and the waves had only been 12 feet high. During severe storms they could reach 20 to 30 feet high.

The Seawall

No, the problem was not the weather, but time. It had been clear for the last two years that the center of Plum Island had been running out of its reservoir of Paleolithic sand and that the groins had been blocking what sand was available from flowing naturally up the beach. So now there was not enough sand for the beach to repair itself after storms like the ones we had last March. We were already paying the price and winter hadn't even arrived in the Northern Hemisphere.

The next day Senator Tarr made a conference call to the manager of the Army Corps of Engineers Piscataqua River dredging project in Portsmouth New Hampshire. It sounded like good news. Plum Island stood to receive 255,000 cubic yards of dredge spoils from the project. All Massachusetts had to do was come up with the $1.1 million dollars in taxpayers money to pay for the polluted sand. Oh and one more detail. The sand wouldn't be ready until 2016.

But Plum Island had a far more basic problem. If Massachusetts really were able to raise the million dollars to dump sand on Plum Island, under the present conditions all that sand would wash away during the next storm. This had already happened after homeowners had scarped the beach in 2012, and again after this minor storm in 2013.

No, Plum Island would have to remove the 1960's groins, before any kind of renourishment project would work. And they only had two years to accomplish the task. How many more houses would be lost in the interim?

Falling loose rocks

CHAPTER 56
BUMMER ON 35TH STREET
December 20, 2013

In late December the Travel Channel invited me to New York to film a piece on horseshoe crabs. We were going to do the segment at the Player's Club, an actor's hangout housed in a palatial Gramercy Park mansion built by the former Shakespearean actor Edwin Booth. The steward of the club told us that Ethan Hawke would be holding a reception that afternoon and showed us the table where Mark Twain used to play poker. Little mention was made of the fact that the former owner's brother had assassinated America's most beloved president.

But that is not the point of our story. The day before the shoot, I walked up 35th Street to buy a big, fat, juicy, hot pastrami sandwich -- the kind you can only find in an authentic New York deli.

As I was picked my way through the crowd mobbing the sidewalk I heard a sharp slap and turned to see that someone had just dropped their shopping bag. It was blowing around in the wind so I grabbed the bag and looked up the street to see who might have lost it. There was a nice little old lady loaded down with shopping bags already churning half a block ahead of me.

As I struggled through the crowds it felt like I was in one of those dreams where you cant move fast enough to get where you want to go. Time seemed to slow down and voices became attenuated. But I did hear someone say "Isn't that nice," and another say "Now you don't see that very often."

I was feeling pretty good about myself. The street was full of the sweet smell of roasting chestnuts and I figured I was about to save someone's Christmas morning. Perhaps they would be telling the story when opening their presents. I not quite sure but I think I heard the sound track of "The Miracle of 34th Street" wafting down from on high. Frank Capra would be proud.

I finally caught up with the elderly lady and tapped her on the shoulder to politely enquire, "Excuse me Ma'am but is this your bag?" She peered into the bag, spied the Macy's package, exclaimed with delight, "No but I'll take it!" and headed up the street too fast for me to follow.

My "Miracle on 34th Street" story had turned into just another "Tale of Two Cities" but we won the pennant, so Merry Christmas New York, and Happy New Year to Boston!

"Remove those groins!"

CHAPTER 57
NEW YEAR'S RESOLUTION
December 27, 2013

In December I drove to Plum Island to get a foretaste of winter. So far, it felt like the calm before the storm. The East Coast hurricane season had been the quietest in almost four decades. Only one storm had made landfall in the United States.

The Pacific was on the opposite extreme. The most powerful storm ever recorded, typhoon Haiyan had just killed 3,660 people and displaced 250 million inhabitants. It had followed two other storms of almost similar strength. The juxtaposition of the two extremes on either side of the globe will keep climatologists scratching their heads for years.

There had been no significant storms in New England since last March, but Plum Island was still a mess. Its beach profile was steep and dangerous and boulders had started tumbling off the face of the emergency seawalls.

If you took a sight line along the front of the beach you could see the problem. The center of the island near the Parker River Wildlife Refuge and the north end of the island near the Merrimack River had recovered from the March storms. They now had the broad plateaus of sand associated with a summer beach.

But the portion of the beach within the groin fields was steep, narrow, and scalloped with erosion. The high tide waves were pounding right up against the seawalls and lashing the house foundations. This part of the beach had not recovered. It still had the steep and narrow profile of a winter beach.

This was the reason that building a sand dune would not work. There was simply not enough beach left to support a sand dune. Storm waves would attack the dunes directly rather than dissipating their energy by running up the face of a natural beach first.

So the very first step of any project to slow down erosion on Plum Island should be to alter or remove these groins. This would allow the beach to straighten itself out naturally and become uniformly broad from the Merrimack River south to the Refuge.

One way to alter the groins would be to refigure them into breakwaters running parallel to the shore. Then, instead of blocking the flow of sand like a groin, the breakwaters would create a protected lee that would encourage sand to collect both in the lee of the breakwaters and more sand to build out from the shore. In just a year's time the beach should become eighty to a hundred feet wider.

Once you had this naturally occurring wider beach, then you could start thinking about restoring the dunes through replanting and beach scraping.

Of course there are no guarantees that refiguring the groins into breakwaters would be enough to save the houses on the primary dune but it would be a significant first step. Plus there are potential funds to do this work.

The Massachusetts legislature has passed the Cantwell bill that provides up to $20 million dollars to remove or repair dams and seawalls. With a little political muscle these funds could be used to also remove or alter groins. The town of Newbury would have to make the request before August 2014.

So I proposed that that the state and town of Newbury make a New Year's resolution to remove the groins on Plum Island by 2015. But something intervened!

The New Year's Storm

CHAPTER 58
THE NEW YEAR'S STORM
January 3, 2014

The first storm of 2014 arrived on January first, then hung around like an unwelcome guest for the next three days. I decided to visit Plum Island during the last of the 10.3-foot high tides. It was expected to be the most damaging of all.

But as I was approaching the island, the sun came out, the wind swung around to the south and the waves dropped from twenty to fifteen feet. All these changes would help homeowners trying to protect their homes.

It was a familiar scene as I entered the island. The high tide had already crawled out of the marsh to cover the causeway in three spots. Utility trucks were busily checking the water hydrants. It made me wonder how the water and sewer lines were faring.

I parked at the Blue Inn and trudged through twenty inches of snow to one of the few lookout areas between the houses on Fordham Way. Clusters of people were perched on steep, ice-covered cliffs of sand above the angry ocean.

Towering surf covered us with freezing spray and battered the fragile sand bank below. Waves had already torn several feet of sand from under the houses on either side of the overlook. Frost seemed to be the only thing keeping the dunes from collapsing into the surf. A large dog strained on his leash to get away from the cliff but his owner urged his daughter to stand on the edge so he could take a good picture.

I decided to move on to the low area where the ocean had broken through a low spot during the last storm. It was a striking sight. Waves were breaking over what was left of the dune where Harry Trout's house had stood only a year before.

Harry was standing in front of his second home directing a snowplow to push together a four-foot high ice dam to block the ocean from flowing across Fordham Way. You could see that this had become a chronic problem. The ocean now flooded into Harry's new lot during every storm.

Harry's problem was that his neighbors had built an emergency seawall after last year's March storm. But Harry had not bothered to spend the $40,000 to extend the seawall across his empty lot. Why should he?

But now, waves were wrapping around the end of his neighbor's seawall and cutting into Harry's former lot. The ocean had already crept ten feet closer to his house and was flowing freely over the water and sewer lines buried under Fordham Way.

The same thing had happened further up the island on Annapolis Way. Except there, waves had already torn 60 feet off Milton Yzitzenikos' empty lot. Milton was the only person who had done the right thing and moved his house across the street. But now he was also getting penalized by his neighbors' seawall that had increased the rate of erosion in front of his relocated home.

Further up the beach the result was the same. Waves were wrapping around the end of the seawall and undermining Bennett Hill. They had already eroded 63 feet off the hill endangering the vulnerable old Bennett Cottage. Now the owners of the cottage had a dilemma. If they extended the seawall across their land it would only move the focus of erosion to their neighbor's lot then on to Center Groin area where the island had almost broken in two in the 1950's. They threatened to sue.

The town had an even more vexing problem. Gaps in the seawall had created three areas where the ocean could flow over the water and sewer mains that were the lifelines of the island. Hurricane Sandy had caused the system to fail a year ago. Who should be responsible for fixing the problem?

The EPA had forced the town to install the water and sewer lines for the homeowners benefit. But it was the homeowners' illegal seawall that was threatening the system and making the island vulnerable to being breached.

Should taxpayers be expected to pay to extend the seawall in front of empty lots? Should the town use the water and sewer betterment to protect the town's lifelines? Should the town sue the homeowners to pay for the damages? Should the state remove the seawalls and groins so the beach would grow wider and protect the island's homes and infrastructure more effectively? Should the town stop encouraging people to rebuild in the dunes?

Before I could answer any of these questions, I was in for one more surprise. As I was driving off the island I noticed that the main road was covered with 6 inches of water. Some had slopped over the street from the marsh, but shop owners said that most of the water was bubbling up through the ground.

A lens of fresh water usually "floats" on the salt water below a barrier beach. Had the high tide pushed the fresh water up through the sand to the surface?

Or was there a simpler explanation? Hurricane Sandy had caused the water system to fail. Had this storm damaged the water and sewer system to fail as well? Would town officials tell me about it if it had? The case against Camp Dresser was still proceeding ahead. Was a new gag order in place? Were Newbury's illegal seawalls threatening Newburyport's jointly owned water and sewer system? Would this put the two neighboring communities at odds?

Perhaps I would get some answers at the town of Newbury's emergency meeting about Plum Island. But first the Plum Island homeowners had to have their say.

When I got home I received a call from Newburyport's Mayor Donna Holladay. She assured me that the city would know if any water mains had been broken. But when I pointed that I had seen utility trucks inspecting the hydrants, she admitted they had encountered a few problems. Apparently the storm had frozen the cans that hold the water main's air vacuum system. Whew, that was a relief.

Dog cringes as father directs his daughter to stand near the edge so he can get a good picture.

The beach in 2013.

The beach in 2014. Because of this seawall Plum Island will never have wide summer beaches again.

CHAPTER 59
MISTAKING THE CAUSE FOR THE CURE
January 7, 2014

After the New Year's storm, homeowners were quick to jump onto the airwaves proclaiming that the "emergency" seawall had protected their homes. It was a familiar scene, six homeowners making the argument that what was good for their homes was good for Plum Island.

But they were confusing the cause with the cure. The seawalls had created two new washover areas, one across Fordham Way, one across Annapolis Way and severe erosion at Bennett Hill. All of these potential new breakthrough areas are at the ends of sections of the seawall.

Storm waves could now wrap around the seawalls and scour sand out from downstream sand dunes. Both Milton Tzitzenikos and Bennett Hill lost 60 feet off their dunes and Harry Trout only a few feet less. A permanent break in any one of the locations would destroy the integrity of the island and leave the other 1200 houses on the island without sewer, water or access.

The homeowners were also misinterpreting what was happening behind the seawalls. Cracks between boulders in the seawall were actually accelerating the waves as they rushed through the structure. This was undermining the seawall causing it to collapse.

This had already happened to Helen Dolberg. Her section of the seawall had slumped allowing waves to rip the porch off her house during the storm. Even the 5-ton concrete blocks along an-

SEAWALLS; MISTAKING THE CAUSE FOR THE CURE

other part of the seawall had started to slump. It was only a matter of time before other sections of the hastily built seawall would also collapse endangering the 30 odd homes behind them.

Homeowners had thrown the seawalls together without putting any fabric behind them to dissipate wave energy. This had been a manmade tragedy, not a natural disaster.

Three VW sized boulders being transported to the jetty.

CHAPTER 60
THE JETTY
January 15, 2014

"The physics of sand is not rocket science.
It is much more complicated than that."
-Albert Einstein's advice to his son, warning him to avoid coastal geology.

The 15th was a bright, sunny, January thaw kind of day. I decided to see if I could catch the beginning of the repair work on the Merrimack River's south jetty. I was in luck. Just as I clambered over the top of the North Point dunes, a huge flatbed truck came lumbering through the dunes on a special road covered with steel plates, the kind General Patton might have used to drive his tanks through the boggy swamps of Italy. The truck was carrying three 5-ton boulders. Several bright yellow excavators were waiting for low tide so they could carefully lift the rocks off the truck and then place them on the jetty.

Homeowners were thrilled. They thought that this $2.5 Million dollar outlay of public funds was going to save their homes, half a mile away.

They were counting on the so-called south flowing current that had supposedly built a half-mile long sandbar that was now focusing erosion on Annapolis Way.

The sandbar was supposed to grow in a cyclical pattern that focused erosion on different parts of the beach in a repeatable way. Unfortunately that convenient myth was wrong.

So how did this myth come about? If you look at charts from the 1800's, as Mike Morris had done, you can see arrows showing that currents flowed from the center of the island north and from the center of the island south. Geologists call these longshore currents because they flow parallel to the shore constantly moving sand up and down the beach. 19th century Newburyport fishermen knew these currents flowed north because they had to row against them to reach their fishing grounds.

But three people and common sense turned this accurate information on its head. Common sense says that if you look at a map, currents will flow south like in the Mississippi River. After all, water flows downhill right?

The three people were a bit more complicated. The first person was Ralph Abele a grad student at U-Mass abetted by Duncan Fitzgerald at Boston University. Abele used an old wind rose to show that Northeast winds set up currents that flow south. Unfortunately his data was based on nearshore winds. But his paper also seemed to make sense.

But that was before we had offshore wave buoys. Now we know that in the beginning of a Northeaster short period waves will approach from the Northeast, but as the storm develops it creates larger long period waves that come directly onto the beach from the East. There might be a few short period waves skidding along on top of the longer period waves but the major swell will be from hitting the shore from the East.

This happens because waves grow deeper as well as higher the longer they travel over the ocean. So when northeast waves near the coast their northern end hits the ocean bottom first and friction causes them to swing around so they end up attacking the shore straight on from the East.

But once a paper such as Abele's is written it becomes part of the scientific record and people keep referring to it until it is proven wrong and often for a long time afterwards as well. If the Army Corps of Engineers had done a proper sand cell analysis before starting the jetty repair they would have discovered that the longshore currents actually flow north, but they might have also lost the contract to do the work.

The second person was Vince Russo, the former head of the Newbury board of selectmen, also known as the mayor of Plum Island. When several houses were being threatened by erosion around 2004, the former surgeon was walking his dog and noticed that the jetty was slumping in several places.

He came to the conclusion that his Northern Boulevard house was in jeopardy because the jetties were in need of repair. Russo was an influential guy and this jibed with his political philosophy -- the reason that people were about to lose their homes was that a large federal bureaucracy in Washington wasn't doing its job.

Russo's theory was also based on the assumption that the longshore currents flowed south and had built up an offshore sandbar that was focusing erosion on successive hotspots.

There are offshore sandbars that do focus waves energy on Plum Island but they are all formed naturally when waves pull sand off the beach during storms. They have nothing to do with a powerful south flowing current. They also tend to migrate back to the beach the following summer.

The final group of people who fostered this common misperception was the Army Corps of Engineers itself. The Corps is required to show that the cost of any project will be less than the benefit to the community. As we have seen, the numbers didn't work out for the Merrimack River if they simply looked at the benefits to navigation. But if they showed that repairing the jetty was going to help prevent erosion on Plum Island they would be in business.

I played an unwitting part of this bureaucratic sleight of hand. I was on the Army Corps of Engineers bus when they were making their pitch to local and state officials traveling from Plum Island to Salisbury Beach. The homeowners Washington lobbyist Howard Marlowe had kept talking about this south flowing current that was causing all the erosion. But when I looked out the window at Central Groin I saw sand building up on the south side of the rocks so the long shore current had to be flowing North.

Finally I tapped one of the friendlier looking engineers on the shoulder and asked, "Isn't this a textbook example of long shore currents moving north?" He put his finger to his lips and whispered quietly, "You are absolutely right. Don't say a word." Being the new kid on the block I didn't say a word, so I suppose I am the fourth person to blame.

So there it was. The jetty was being repaired and homeowners were convinced that once it is done by the March 31st due date, their problems would be over. Unfortunately, they had forgotten that March 31st is followed by April Fools Day.

Like beach scraping, seawalls, groins, Geotubes and all the other hard engineering solutions, that had been tried, the jetty repair wasn't going to make a particle of difference either. They had been fooled once again.

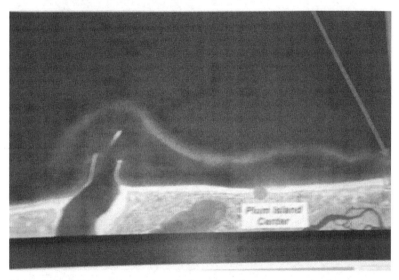

Jetties push sand into deeper water where it can no longer protect the shore.
Pita Photo Courtesy Mike Morris

The Bennets lost 60 feet because of their neighbor's seawall.

CHAPTER 61
THE TRIFECTA;
January 17, 2014

On January 9th homeowners convinced the Newbury Board of Selectmen to declare Plum Island to be a state of emergency. They felt that this would force the DEP to allow the homeowners to put more rocks on the seawalls that had caused the problem in the first place.

I visited the island a few days later and was saddened by what I saw. Six houses were now only one storm or several high tides from being washed away. This was three more houses than when I had been on the beach only nine days before and we hadn't had any storms or particularly high tides. The damage was due to failure of the poorly designed seawalls. Scouring in the gaps and at the ends of the seawalls had also created three areas where the ocean could break through the dunes, undermine the waters lines and clog the sewer vents in a deep bowl behind the first tier of houses.

We had a few brief meetings of our Storm Surge group and Mike Morris wrote a letter to the editor and I wrote the following article suggesting that the towns of Newbury and Newburyport form a blue ribbon panel to plan for the long-term future of Plum Island. It seemed like it was worth a try:

Plum Island is about to win the Trifecta. If you open any textbook on coastal geology, you will see that the three best ways to increase erosion on a beach are to build a groin, install a seawall or repair a jetty.

The state built the Fordham, Annapolis and Central groins in the 1960's, homeowners built the Great Wall of Newbury in 2012 and the Army Corps of Engineers will finish repairing the South Jetty in 2014.

We have already seen the results. The groins caused 6 houses to topple over the edge and 40 more to be condemned; the seawall is collapsing along its entire length and has already failed in 6 locations.

Scour in the gaps and ends of the seawall have created three new potential breakthrough areas that threaten the island's jointly owned sewer and water system. When the jetty is complete it will jeopardize many of the North Point structures and do nothing for the homes on Annapolis and Fordham Ways.

All these mistakes were made by well-intentioned, likable people who thought they were doing the right thing. But they have jeopardized the integrity of the island and sealed the fate of up to a hundred homes.

So what should we do now? There is nothing we can do for most of the homes in the primary dunes south of Central Groin. The same is true for most of the structures north of South Jetty.

What we can do, is start the long arduous process of changing how we think about living on an island beside the ocean. We have to stop believing we can beat the North Atlantic and learn to live with her on her own terms. That means accepting the fact that ocean waves are going to continue to break on Plum Island. There is nothing we can do about that, but we can learn how to encourage those same waves to rebuild the beach after every storm.

This means realizing you cant build a house on a primary dune and expect either the house or dune to last. This means realizing that you cant build jetties, groins and seawalls and not expect them to change the dynamics of the beach so that erosion is increased elsewhere. This means realizing that barrier beaches are like living entities that need to be able to move, pulsate and grow.

As soon as we make these cultural changes we can start to do things to protect the integrity of the island. These might include stopping building houses in primary dunes to get people out of harm's way. They might include removing or altering the groins so the beach can repair itself.

Just doing that one thing would widen the beach by as much as 80 to 100 feet in the first year. Once the groins are removed renourishing the beach with well-placed sand will start to work effectively rather than just washing away.

We probably have to fill in the gaps in the seawall with properly designed structures and fabric backing to stop waves from undermining the wall and boulders. We should remove the remains of the seawalls once the houses in the primary dunes collapse. We probably also have to continue repairing the jetty simply because the project is already started and is needed for navigational purposes.

We also need to think of other ways of earning income for the upkeep of one of the most beautiful beaches in New England. These might include charging a toll to cross the Plum Island turnpike, the way they do on so many barrier islands in Florida. These solutions might include charging visitors to park in municipal lots and or use shuttle buses from the train station to the beach, the way they do in Manchester and Ipswich.

Salisbury Beach to the north and Crane's Beach to the south make hundreds of thousands of dollars every summer from parking revenue. These revenues will start to make up for tax revenues lost from not encouraging people to build in the barrier dunes.

The items are endless but the first thing we have to do is stop simply declaring an emergency every year and start thinking of long terms ways we can continue live with the ocean. The way to do that is for the towns of Newbury and Newburyport to form a blue ribbon panel to start to plan for the future of Plum Island.

The beach shuddered as the boulders rolled out of the dump trucks.

Chapter 62
FILLING IN THE GAPS
January 20, 2014

All New England paused in January to watch the Denver Broncos eviscerate our once proud Patriots. It was depressing to watch. One by one our players limped off the field, leaving our defense unable to stop a pass, our offense never on the field long enough to throw the ball.

But our biggest enemy was the clock. Minute by minute it wound down while Tom Brady sat helpless on the bench. Minute by minute the Broncos watched our collapse, while the high mountain air sucked the energy out of our players until the humiliating defeat was finally over.

The next day I decided to see how Plum Island's seawall repairs were going. It was probably not a good idea, so soon after the championship game.

As far as anyone could tell, the state of Massachusetts had not approved any repair work, but the homeowners were using Newbury's emergency declaration to go ahead anyway. It had snowed the day the Beachcoma had held a benefit to shore up Bennett Hill. But nobody had made a bid on the Patriot's tickets and the event had only raised $9,000. It was going to cost a whole lot more than that to save the hill.

But by Monday a fleet of trucks, excavators, and Bob Cats were dumping piles of huge rocks on the beach then going back for more. The beach trembled as tons of rocks crashed onto the sand.

Workers were on their knees rolling out large pieces of erosion fabric on the slope of Bennett Hill. At least this was an improvement over what had been done in March.

One excavator stood poised at the bottom of the hill. It passed heavy boulders up to another excavator half way up the slope. Then they would act in tandem to position each boulder onto the sand dune before going back for more. They looked like a pair of towering Brontosauri tenderly placing eggs in their nest before covering it with sand.

The same thing was happening all along the beach. Homeowners were ripping up the old seawalls they had built in March and starting all over again with larger rocks and much more fabric. Sometimes the work was being done in front of houses that were technically uninhabitable because the ocean had already torn away their second exit.

But nothing was being done in front of the Tzitzenikos lot that needed it the most. The ocean was now three feet closer to undermining the sewer line than it had been only 5 days before.

The problem was money. While the homeowners were willing to spend up to $80,000 to remain in their houses for another season, the town of Newbury didn't have the money to ensure the safety of the island for the next ten years.

It was like watching the Patriots all over again. The homeowners were trying every strategy in the book, but the ocean was grinding them down. They only have a few minutes left on the clock. The sea has an eternity.

The excavators looked Brontosaurii building their nests.

Waves breaking on the offshore sandbar.

CHAPTER 63
SAND CELLS ON THE SEASHORE
January 27, 2014

On January 27th I drove to Plum Island in near darkness to meet with Ron Barrett. Ron is one of the most knowledgeable people on Plum Island, but forget trying to e-mail him. He is a strictly, straight-talking, cell phone kind of guy. What you have to do is catch him on the beach in the morning before he goes to work, or at night after he has just finished delivering heavy-duty materials for the Ron Barrett Construction Transport Company.

But Ron's real job is caring for the island through the Plum Island Taxpayers Association. Unlike most of the island spokesmen, Ron is concerned about saving the entire island rather than half a dozen homes in the primary dunes. And he knows the two goals are quite different.

I am always sure that Ron is going to disagree with everything I say, but am sometimes surprised to discover we are on the same page. During our after-dark seminar Ron told me that he thought the state should have encouraged homeowners to build artificial sand dunes and was griped that they had allowed the illegal seawalls. I agreed but said that I didn't think the sand dunes would have worked.

"Of course they wouldn't have worked, but at least you wont have this damn big pile of rocks sitting on the beach after all the houses wash away."

I said I thought it was a mistake that the Newbury board of Selectmen declared Plum Island a state of emergency twice in two years. It was a little like the boy who cried wolf. The only real building damage you could point to, was that one homeowner had lost her front porch.

We agreed that the homeowners' knew that real emergency had been that their seawalls were already collapsing after only ten months. They argued that they needed the state of emergency so they could fill in the gaps and protect Bennett Hill, but what they really wanted to do was add more rocks to their own sections of the seawall. We also agreed that most of the rocks were too small and that waves would end up throwing them back through the owners' windows during storms.

Ron came down to the site every night to make sure that the contractors picked up all the grapefruit sized pieces of rocks strewn on the beach by the day's work. He didn't want any pieces of sharp rocks lying on the beach after the houses were gone.

We admired the covered sign that Ron made that welcomes visitors to the beach, and discussed the matting Ron planned to place over the extension of the seawall so the public could get to the beach next summer. Ron walked the walk, as well as talked the talk. He reminded me of Dr. Thieler in Woods Hole.

It was almost high tide but we could see the surf breaking over the prominent new sand bar that stretched across the center island. We agreed it was probably providing more protection to the homeowners than their extra-legal seawall.

Ron was a former surfer so I expected that he would credit the elusive south flowing offshore current with building the sandbar, but he fooled me again. He knew that sand flowed north along this section of the beach.

The offshore sandbar was also caused by this north flowing system of waves and currents. Coastal geologists like to talk about an underwater river of sand that shadows what is happening onshore but on a longer time scale and over a larger area.

In the same way that low energy waves pull a few grains of sand off the beach and transport them several inches up the beach all summer. During winter storms, high-energy waves pull large quantities of sand off the beach and store them in these off-shore sandbars. In the spring, longer period waves then transport the sand back to the beach but several yards down from where it had been the winter before.

Over several years this underwater river will move the sand all the way down the beach from the center of the island to the jetty where much of it will be shot out into deeper water and lost to the system.

Geologists call this system a sand cell. It consists of all the sand that is constantly being moving north in both the underwater river of sand and along the beach by waves and currents. So this new sandbar was made from the massive pulse of sand that erod-ed out of the Parker River Refuge during last winter's storms. In a few short years it will be at the jetty.

But I will have to return to the beach after dark to see if Ron agrees. If not, I know he will let me know in no uncertain terms.

The sewer line is now behind 60 feet of rock and sand. This house is on the far side of Annapolis Way where the sewer line is buried.

CHAPTER 64
MOVE IT OR LOSE IT
February 14, 2014

On February 14th I revisited Plum Island. It was the day after
a massive storm abetted by the misbehaving Polar Vortex had
killed 21 people, dropped more than a foot of snow on the East
Coast, and left 1.2 million homeowners without power from Florida
to Maine. The storm would continue to gain strength from the ab-
normally warm Atlantic and go on to pummel the U.K. and Europe,
which were already experiencing the worst flooding in memory.

On the other side of the Polar Vortex, California was in its worst
drought in 500 years. It was 60 degrees in Alaska and the Voice
of Russia was gloating over the spring-like weather at the winter
Olympics in Sochi.

Despite the one-liners of climate deniers, these problems were
all caused by global warming. It had heated up the area above
the Arctic Circle so much that there was no longer a barrier between the cold air in the north and the warm air in the south. This
allowed the Jet Stream to swoop down deeply into North American Continent to spread its havoc. It was yet another sign, that our
climate is in the throes of deep distress. This is a variation of the
madhouse world that scientists had warned of back in the 1970's.

By the time I reached Plum Island the radio pundits were already referring to the storm in the past tense. But apparently the
island had been listening to another station. Snow was blowing
sideways in forty-knot winds and ten-foot waves were crashing
hallway up the seawall and sucking out sand from beneath the
new structure. Their backwash had a brownish gray muddy color –

the color of water supersaturated with suspended sand. Although it was providing immediate protection to the houses, only a few more storms would see the seawall collapse like its predecessor.

The homeowners were saying that the seawall was their last and best defense. They sounded like unlucky gamblers just before the casino was about to close. They had been losing all night long but knew that if they just bet the mortgage, they would surely win back all their earnings.

But Milton Tzitzenikos had adopted another strategy. He had decided to fold and leave the casino while he still owned his home.

His neighbors had each spent $80,000 to build and rebuild the seawall in front of their homes, while Milton had opted to spend only $30,500 to move his home to the other side of the street. With luck and a good hand, he would be able to continue to enjoy his ocean view for many more years to come.

The same could not be said for the other homeowners who had just gambled that they could spend another $80,000 and save their homes that were now worth less than $250,000.

The Atlantic Ocean made this fragile barrier beach and lent it to humans for a few hundred years. But now it was her turn to play and she wanted her island back. It is becoming clear that it is not a good bet to gamble against the Atlantic Ocean. She owns the house.

The view from the proposed new house site.

CHAPTER 65
GREAT DESIGN, LOUSY LOCATION
February 18, 2014

Ross Westcott was nervous. The former candidate for the
Newbury Conservation Commission was making a pitch to build
his own house on Fordham Way. It would be the last item on the
night's long agenda. Marilyn winced as Ross stepped outside to
smoke his third cigarette of the evening.

The agenda reflected the dilemma facing the commission. Six
of the ten items before the committee had to do with building new
homes or modifying existing homes on Plum Island. That meant
that close to 60% of all the construction in town was taking place
on this narrow little strip of sand with urban density. And some
would argue that no development should be allowed there anyway,
because Plum Island homes had such a propensity for toppling
into the ocean.

An onlooker would be forgiven for thinking he had wandering
into the building inspector's meeting by mistake. All commissioners had been in the construction business and most had been on
the board for years, if not decades. The measures were all being
passed unanimously and the only discussion was about how to
build the houses, not if they should be built in the first place.

The meeting finally came to Ross's proposal. He had put a
great deal of time into drawing up plans for his new home. It
would be round instead of angular and built around a central pole.
He had done away with a garage and elevated the house so he
could grow dune grass in the house's shadow. He had done a
sunlight analysis and hired the best dune grass specialist in New
England to make sure the native plants would thrive. He had

also elevated the house so the dune could move freely below the rainwater irrigation system underneath the modernesque structure. It was one of the most environmentally friendly plans for a house designed to be built on a dune, where people are normally prohibited from walking.

Ross had a great design, but a lousy location. The Westcotts were proposing to build their dream house across the street from where three houses had washed away less than ten months before. It was right beside Harry Trout's lot that was flooded with ocean water during every storm and it was on Fordham Way, where ocean waves were threatening to undermine the Newbury sewer line and break the island in two.

One of Ross's neighbors, Jane Peng, made an eloquent plea that the Conservation Commission declare a moratorium on building any new houses in this flood prone section of Plum Island. It was a reasonable suggestion. But the conservation agent said he wasn't sure that the commission could even declare a moratorium, to the shaking of sage heads and murmurs of agreement. It was like the scene in Pirates of the Caribbean where Jack Sparrow asks if any of the pirates had ever sailed with Captain Barbarossa setting off a chorus of "Nope not me's" and "Never heard of the guy."

But such moratoriums are commonplace in Massachusetts. Falmouth, Nantucket and Chatham passed similar moratoria on building any more houses and seawalls on sensitive areas.

But moratoria only make sense if they are coupled with a committee tasked with planning for new ways of living beside the Atlantic Ocean. Such a blue ribbon panel would also help get the town of Newbury and the commissioners off the horns of their dilemma. Instead of declaring a state of emergency one week then giving permissions to build new houses the next, they could start planning for the future, rather than making more problems for the future.

CHAPTER 66
THE TROUBLE WITH
FLOOD INSURANCE
Massachusetts March 7, 2014

Margaret Motyl dreaded every winter. Not for herself, she lives in Florida, but for her second home in Scituate, Massachusetts. She and Gary bought their house in 2007 for $1.2 Million dollars. It looked safe enough, sitting behind a concrete seawall that had been rebuilt several times since its 1906 installation. But looks can be deceiving.

The 1978 Blizzard had knocked the house off its foundation and the ocean had poured through a gash in the roof during The Perfect Storm in 1991. In fact the house had been destroyed and rebuilt nine times at taxpayers expense for over three quarters of a million dollars.

Part of the problem was that the concrete seawall that gave a false sense of security. It looked reassuring in the summer but it created more problems than it solved in the winter.

Within a few years of the seawall's installation, the beach had steepened and waves richocheting off its base had washed all the sand out to sea. The ocean then lapped against the crumbling seawall at every high tide and grapefruit sized rocks were all that remained of the beach. During storms surf would blast these perfectly sized projectiles up over the walls and through peoples' plate glass windows.

But Margaret didn't have to worry. The government had helped the former owner of her house reinforce the front walls with 2-by 8's and replace the windows with bulletproof glass.

The government also paid $40,000 to elevate the house and now Margaret wanted to see if it would pay another $80,000 to elevate it again. Not that she needed the money. Her late husband had been chief financial officer of the Templeton Global Equity Group. But she was perfectly within her rights to apply for the government largess.

That is the problem with the federal flood insurance program. It was designed to help people but now it just encourages people to do things like install seawalls and rebuild houses where the ocean wants to be.

"The Bio Station", Bermuda.

CHAPTER 67
THE ANSWER MY FRIEND,
IS BLOWIN IN THE WIND.
March 24, 2014

In mid-March I hopped on a plane for Bermuda, only to wait an hour for the ground crew to de-ice our plane in what people mistakenly thought was the last snowstorm of the season.

I thought I was getting away from all the hoopla about whether President Obama would sign the bill to water down flood insurance reform. Little did I realize that I was flying right into the eye of the storm.

Bermuda is the capital of the re-insurance industry. If you want to impress your billionaire friends just drop the hint that your hedge fund is in Bermuda's offshore re-insurance business. It is the ultimate status symbol. Only the highest of the high rollers can afford the volatile risks of the re-insurance game. After all, you are betting against the weather.

The re-insurance industry is one of those shadowy little fix-it businesses that makes capitalism work. It is not for the impecunious or the faint of heart.

What the re-insurance industry does is provide insurance to insurance companies. Without it the insurance industry would have gone belly up when hurricanes started becoming more frequent back in the early 1990's.

Karen Clark was several months pregnant when she first visited Lloyds of London in 1987 to argue that the insurance industry didn't have a clue how close they were to disaster. She hauled out her clunky old laptop that showed that a single storm could topple the insurance industry, but because the Atlantic had been in a 30-year period of low hurricane activity nobody had paid much attention.

The masters of the universe smiled politely, but didn't bother to ask any questions. Why should they listen to some newly minted grad student when they had been in the business for 30 years?

But that was exactly what Karen was trying to tell them. They had made all their money during the 30-lull in hurricane activity. They hadn't been smart. They had been lucky.

Karen was vindicated in 1992 when Hurricane Andrew slammed into Miami on August 24th. Insurance executives were apoplectic. They assumed they might lose a few billion bucks on such a storm, but AIR, Karen's Boston based research firm had sent them all faxes of her catastrophe model results that showed they stood to lose over $13 Billion dollars. It turned out they lost $15.5 Billion. The storm put "cat modeling" on the map.

There are two kinds of practitioners of the dark art of betting against the wind. Those that bet a hurricane will arrive and those who bet that it wont.

Brian Hunter was the first type. In the summer of 2005 he noticed that American refineries had large supplies of natural gas and the cost of the valuable commodity was low. But nobody was buying options on the gas because they thought its cost would stay low.

The high living young commodity trader bought trillions of cubic feet of the valuable gas for millions of dollars. It looked like a foolhardy trade until hurricane Katrina swept through the Gulf of Mexico killing 1,833 people and leaving the city of New Orleans underwater.

Katrina had also overturned a hundred oil rigs and driven the price of gas through the roof. Hunter earned himself a $131 million dollar bonus and made his company rich. Not bad for a 31 year old kid from Calgary.

But like his less colorful colleagues in Lloyd's of London he too started to believe he was smart, not just lucky. A few years later he lost $8 Billion dollars of his clients money when the price of natural gas didn't rise as it usually did during the summer months.

John Seo was the other type of trader. His career had taken a curious detour after graduating from MIT in physics, earning a PhD in Biophysics from Harvard and landing a teaching assistant job at Brandeis. His wife became pregnant and the Brandeis health insurance policy wouldn't cover what it determined was a preexisting condition.

So John signed up for an eight-week stint with a trading company just so they could get health insurance. But when he finished the temporary job the head of the company offered him a $40,000 bonus and a $250,000 starting salary just to stay on.

John's mother wept when she heard the news. For this, she had walked out of North Korea and earned the first PhD in math even given to a Korean woman? For this, she had worked in a donut shop to earn money so her son could go to MIT? John's father was more direct, "The devil has come as a prostitute and asked you to lie down with her. " It was probably not the typical response of an American family learning that their son had just been hired to work on Wall Street.

John, however, was not destined to have a typical Wall Street career. He became obsessed with figuring out what an insurance company should charge to insure against an extremely unlikely financial event like the value of the dollar falling by a third in one year. He had become what Wall Streeters call a tail pricer, someone who figures out the risk of an event occurring at the tail end of a bell-shaped probability curve.

Word got around that this nerdy kid was pretty good at tail pricing so Leman Brothers was soon knocking on his door offering him a job to figure out how much an insurance company should charge to cover losses from a hundred year storm.

The more John looked at the problem the more he realized Karen Clark had been right. A single storm could topple the insurance industry. Why, even a government subsidized Flood Insurance program of a wealthy country like the United States could be vulnerable. Wall Street was the only place where you could find people willing to gamble that they could make enough money during years without hurricanes to offset years with hundred year storms.

Seo became so sure of the social benefit of offering this kind of insurance to insurance companies that he quit Leman Brothers to start his own hedge fund. He named it after his hero the French mathematician Pierre de Fermat. Fermat's specialty would be catastrophe bonds. Cat bonds were bonds that cover insurers losses during a disaster like hurricane Katrina but bonds that also pay high yields from premiums paid during years without storms.

2013 had been such a year. There had been no hurricanes to speak of and premiums had been set high because insurance were willing to pay high premiums because they remembered the losses they had sustained during Sandy and Irene the year before. But was 2013 a bellwether year?

That was the $64 Billion dollar question. Would the gods that determine the North Atlantic weather system give us 30 years of frequent hurricanes like the period from 1991 to 2012, or 30 years with infrequent storms like the years from 1961 to 1991?

Scientists call these climatological gods El Nino and the North Atlantic Oscillation and when they work in unison it means that people like John Seo can make a ton of money for his investors.

It made pretty good mathematical sense. But it also pointed out that countries like the United States have areas of concentrated wealth along its coasts that defy the logic of insurance. And that this system of insurance and re-insurance, as kludgy as it may seem, is probably also the best way to protect against catastrophic hurricane losses.

If the United States had never entered the flood insurance business hundreds of thousands of people would not have been encouraged to build homes beside flood prone rivers and on vulnerable barrier beach islands, because they would not have been able to afford the rates commercial flood insurance could afford to give them. And places like Plum Island would still be beach communities with only a few houses situated where they could afford commercial flood insurance provided only for once in a lifetime catastrophe.

The logic of insurance seemed to make so much sense, but on the day we returned home, President Obama signed the bill delaying flood insurance reform. People who had been flooded 25 times in 25 years had won. They had convinced their Congressmen to kick the bottle down the road until the next big storm, or the next big election, whichever came first.

So perhaps long-term investors like John Seo are better at knowing which way the wind is blowing than Congressmen concerned about getting elected every other year.

March 10, 2013

CHAPTER 68
TWO PATHS TOWARD THE FUTURE
May 16, 2014

One of the most striking features of Plum Island is how different the beach looks in Newbury than it does Newburyport. In Newbury the ocean crashes up against illegal seawalls built to protect homes on Fordham and Annapolis Ways. In Newburyport, there is almost a football field worth of dune grass and primary dunes between the northernmost houses and the ocean.

Part of this has to do with geology. The houses in Newbury are near the center of the sand cell where sand is eroding, but Newburyport is at the end of the sand cell where sand is accumulating. If you want to build a house on a beach it is always better to build it where the sand is growing, not where it is eroding.

The other reason that the situation is so different in the two communities has to do with politics, administration and economics. Newbury is a small, cash strapped rural town. The only section of the community that is heavily developed is her half of Plum Island that has a constricted urban density. So only about 3% of the town's land area accounts for 40% of her tax revenue.

Newburyport, on the other hand, is a moderate sized city that concentrates on its riverside waterfront and urban problems. She tends to regard her section of Plum Island as a world apart, a small, funky neighborhood of mostly summer homes that only supplies a small portion of the city's total tax revenues. So many newly divorced men live there that locals call it, "Man Island".

These geographic facts effect how the two communities regard their sections of Plum Island. Newbury thinks of Plum Island as an all-important cash cow that must be kept residential so the money will keep flowing in. But, Newburyport is free to take a more responsible view of its section of Plum Island because she is less dependent on it for tax revenue.

Like most Massachusetts communities, Newburyport is strict about allowing adverse impacts to its dunes and beach. This also frees up Newburyport to think of her portion of Plum Island as having an economic worth based more on being an island with a clean accessible public beach rather than a place to build houses.

Newburyport's section of Plum Island also has room for two moderate-sized parking lots that provide immediate summertime revenue. This is added to the multiplier effect of having beach goers and renters buy food, drink, and fishing tackle at local establishments.

In the future, Newbury will probably continue to privatize its beaches and overdevelop its dunes, while Newburyport will continue to evolve more toward a beach-based economy. There are many close examples of communities that have successfully taken that route.

To the north, Salisbury Beach brings in over $250,000 a summer from parking fees, while to the south, Crane's Beach does the same thing charging as much as $20 a day for each car. Ipswich and Manchester have buses that shuttle people and their bikes from the train station to their beaches. Newburyport could do the same and even charge a small toll for using the Plum Island causeway to enter the island the way similar communities do in Florida.

All of these sources of income could help Newburyport replace any revenue lost from development with money gained from having one of the most beautiful beaches in New England for fishing, swimming and surfing. Who knows, if Newburyport can do it Newbury might even follow in the footsteps of her younger sister, once removed.

CHAPTER 69
THE UNRAVELING
May 28, 2014

On May 28th Bruce Tarr convened the first regional meeting
of the Massachusetts Coastal Erosion Commission in Glouces-
ter. The Senator hoped this would be his crowning achievement.
He had raised money for the panel to advance his belief that the
state's environmental regulations should be relaxed in order to
allow Massachusetts citizens to stop erosion.

Plum Island was going to be his case study. He had hand-se-
lected Newbury's Conservation agent Doug Packer to serve on
the 13-man commission and invited Bob Connors to represent
Plum Island's homeowners.

The three men had done this dozens of times, complain that the
state wasn't giving homeowners permission to protect their homes,
go on television to drum up sympathy, get the Newbury Board of
Selectmen to declare a state of emergency, have Doug Packer
back them up, then build an artificial sand dune, repair a jetty or
construct an illegal seawall knowing that Senator Tarr would make
sure they didn't get caught or fined.

But something wasn't working as planned. This wasn't the
Merrimack River Beach User's Association or the Newbury Board
of Selectmen. The other commission members weren't buying
the Plum Island story as they told it. By law, the commission had
to include professionals; geologists, engineers, state officials
and representatives from environmental organizations. People

like Rob Thieler from the Woods Hole Oceanographic Institution, Bruce Carlisle head of the state's Coastal Zone Management Office and Jack Clarke representative from the Massachusetts Audubon Society.

Bruce Carlisle read off the statistics, Plum Island had lost a hundred feet of beach in the last twenty years. In 2012, 20 feet had washed away during each of the winter's four storms that also destroyed 7 homes and made another 39 uninhabitable. And in just the past six months, the state itself had lost 30 feet of coastline.

Jack Clarke made the point that beaches have to be able to move and that building structures like the massive stone jetties at the mouth of the Merrimack River and the seawalls built on Plum Island only shifted sand offshore increasing the natural rate of erosion. He noted that spending millions of dollars to pump sand on eroding beaches was wasteful, ineffective, and often destructive as well.

Bob Connors was left pretty much speechless. He was used to being able to control the message but all he could do was blame the state for letting nature run its course, saying, "This is America. We don't retreat. We stand, we defend and protect our homes and families."

It made for a great sound byte but it didn't make much sense. People have always retreated in the face of unstoppable natural forces and armies have always made tactical retreats in order to win strategic battles, think Dunkirk and Normandy in which America played a small part if I am not mistaken.

Bob's testimony was really just another sign that the official Plum Island story was unraveling and that Mother Nature would win in the end. She always does.

EPILOGUE
ALTERNATE FUTURES
Plum Island

I grew up in a community very much like Plum Island, with houses on a barrier beach and the mainland. During the last twenty years the barrier beach has broken through twice, twenty-four houses have washed out to sea and nine other houses have been swept off the mainland.

I see the same future for Plum Island. In the next twenty years, I expect that of the thirty-nine houses that were condemned during the 2012 storms will collapse and not be rebuilt. The island will break in two; either at the Basin, Central Groin or Fordham Way. The resulting inlet will grow to about a quarter of a mile wide and migrate another half a mile south destroying more island homes and allowing ocean waves to start battering houses on Plum Island Sound, the Basin, Joppa Flats and in downtown Newburyport.

This will probably not happen in a single storm, but because of cumulative damage caused by a series storms as happened in last year in October, December, February and March, in 2011 and 2012.

The scenario will be roughly the same for all of the other 200 barrier beach islands on the East Coast and the Gulf of Mexico. This will happen even if we could stop emitting all greenhouse gases tomorrow. The future is already built into the system because of the existing amount of carbon dioxide in the atmosphere that will not dissipate for a hundred years. This is not to say that we shouldn't do everything we can to reduce carbon emissions, but that we have a problem that we have to deal with -- right now.

This scenario is not the end of the world. It is still a manageable situation. But it is also one that will require that we adopt new ways of thinking as we adapt to this new reality. We are not going to be able to engineer ourselves out of this situation. Our old system of building hard solutions like jetties groins and seawalls has not worked. It usually made erosion much worse.

But I also believe that there is room for optimism in this future. Climate change is starting to make people appreciate the beauty and recurring resiliency of nature. We are starting to realize that if we want to continue to live on the coasts we have to reverse over two hundred years of mismanagement. But as we start looking for ways to do this, we are discovering that nature has been doing it for eons.

Plants, animals and natural forces have an innate ability to migrate to a damaged area, thrive and heal the wound. It is like nature's own immune system. We see it time and again, after fires, volcanoes, floods and storms.

I remember returning to a Cape Cod beach that had been destroyed, and not being able to tell if I was on the right beach. But gradually I realized a house had once stood where now there were only waves and water. The beach had retreated sixty feet and rebuilt itself naturally, until it looked exactly like it had only a month before.

I have seen places like Cape Cod's Pleasant Bay undergo the equivalent of fifty years of sea level rise overnight and you could barely tell anything had happened only a year later. The marshes had simply grown six inches into the mainland and the bay was cleaner and twice as productive as before.

I have motored through thousands of square acres of marsh-
lands after the BP spill and been unable to see any evidence of
damage. We also remember that the catch of shrimp doubled
the year after that spill. The lesson? If you leave nature alone its
natural fecundity will help it recover.

Now communities all over the world are starting to learn how to
live with water. They are moving people out of dangerous floodplains, widening rivers and planting trees to soak up floodwaters,
marshes to tampen down storm surges and oysters to build up
living breakwaters. They are removing old groins and jetties and
letting beaches widen themselves.

It will not be an easy undertaking. But we have a golden opportunity to start reversing an outmoded mindset and to undo two
hundred years of past mistakes. But if we start to take the first
steps, nature will do the rest for us.

Bill Sargent Ipswich, MA
2014

Alternate Futures.

Notes

FOREWORD

The Well From Hell; Sargent, William, Strawberry Hill Press. Ipswich, MA, 2011. This book chronicles the BP spill and describes the condition of Louisiana's marshes and fisheries a year after the spill.

INTRODUCTION

Storm Surge; A Coastal Village Battles the Rising Atlantic. Sargent, William, University Press of New England, Hanover, NH, 2004. This book chronicles the town of Chatham's battles to combat the effects of sea level rise.

CHAPTER 1 GERRI'S LOSS

Most of these chapters appeared as articles in the Newburyport Current a week after the date of the incident.

The View from Strawberry. Sargent, William, Strawberry Hill Press, Ipswich, MA, 2013. This book chronicles 2012, the hottest year on record.

The Plum Island Talking Points; Marlowe and Company, Washington D.C.

CHAPTER 2 PLUM ISLAND

The House on Ipswich Marsh. Sargent, William, Lebanon NH, 2005, UPNE.com. This book describes the geological history of Plum Island.

Plum Island, As it Was. Weare, Nancy, 1996. This book describes the social history of Plum Island.

CHAPTER 3 THE MERRIMACK RIVER

Personal communication Jerry Klima, Yankee Clipper Cruise, 2013 Newburyport, Wikipedia

CHAPTER 4 SEA LEVEL RISE

Residents must surrender to the sea, author says. Plumb, Taryn, Boston Globe, October 4, 2012.

CHAPTER 5 SUPERSTORM SANDY

In storm deaths, mystery, fate and bad timing. N.R. Kleinfeld, Michael Powell, New York Times October 31, 2013.

CHAPTER 6 COASTAL TRIAGE

Coastal triage. Sargent, William, The Star-Ledger, Trenton, New Jersey 2013

CHAPTER 7 CATALYST FOR CHANGE

The Effects of Hurricane Sandy in New Jersey; Wikipedia.

CHAPTER 8 THE BLIZZARD OF 2013

Ordeal in the snow; Northeast drivers stranded for hours in Blizzard. Frank Eltman, AP February 9, 2013.

CHAPTER 9 AN UNNECESSARY TRAGEDY

Storm devastating to Plum Island. Baker, Billy, Boston Globe March 9 2013.

Storm claims 3 houses. Cerullo, Mac, Newburyport Daily News, March 9, 2013.

CHAPTER 10 COME HELL OR HIGH WATER

It's move it or lose it in path of Northeaster. Bidgood, Jess, New York Times, March 18, 2013.

CHAPTER 11 THE END OF A CONVENIENT MYTH

Plum Island homeowners ignore state regulations, shore up homes. Gellerman, Bruce, Boston Globe, March 22, 2013

CHAPTER 12 THE MEETING

Beach mining moves forward. Hendrickson, Dyke, Newburyort Daily News April 5, 2013.

CHAPTER 13 THE PROPOSAL

Just seconds From the Ocean. Sargent, William, Lebanon, NH, UPNE.com 2008. This book travels along the East and Gulf coasts looking at coastal problems.

CHAPTER 14 WORKING WITH NATURE

How LA neighborhood of the Stars is struggling to Survive James Nye, Daily Mail, UK March 31, 2013.

Broad Beach project runs over budget. Tallal, James, Malibu Times, May 17, 2013.

CHAPTER 15 NOBODY CARES WHAT ACTORS THINK!

State Allows Beach Mining on Plum Island Beach, Hendrickson, Dyke, Newburyport Daily News, April 17, 2013.

CHAPTER 16 A TURNING POINT?

Fate of Plum Island homes uncertain. Tyne, Victor, Newburyport Daily News, March 17, 2010.

CHAPTER 18 A THE RUBBER STAMP

Homeowners to be bought out by the State. CBS News February 25, 2013. Fresh Kills Landfill, Wikipedia.

CHAPTER 19 A WIN-WIN SITUATION

Prince Harry's Jersey Shore Visit, Serrano, Ken, New Jersey Daily Record, May 13, 2013.

NOTES

CHAPTER 21 ROCKS FOR JOCKS

State Blocks Rebuilding of Plum Island House, Hendrikson, Dyke, Newburyport Daily News, May 15, 2013.

CHAPTER 22 HARRY TROUT

No partisan fire at the shore, Stearnes, Michael, Leibovich, Mark, New York Times May 28, 2013.

Obama Christie Bromance, Feldman, Linda, Christian Science Monitor, May 28, 2013.

CHAPTER 23 THE BROMANCE

Crab Wars; A Tale of Horseshoe Crabs, Bioterrorism and Human Health. Sargent, William, Lebanon NH, UPNE.com, 2002. Personal communication Pat Corin, Tim Kennedy American Littoral Society, May 2013.

CHAPTER 24 THE LIFE YOU SAVE MAY BE YOUR OWN

Unprecedented Changes Occur Offshore at Plum Island. Macone, John, Newburyport Daily News, May 21, 2013. A Look Back at Plum Island. Plante, Bill, Newburyport Daily News, May 2013.

CHAPTER 25 GROINS ON A BEACH

Pacific Legal Foundation website Conservation conditions put on Plum Island. WCVB June 4, 2013. DEP may intervene on Plum Island, Hendrickson Dyke, Newburyport Daily News June 3 2013. Pacific Legal Foundation letter to Richard Sullivan, Secretary, Executive Office of Energy and Environmental Affairs for the Commonwealth of Massachusetts. May 29, 2013.

CHAPTER 27 MICHAEL BLOOMBERG

Bloomberg outlines $20 billion storm prevention plan, Gregory, Kia; Satora, Marc; New York Times, June 11, 2013.

CHAPTER 28 THE LEGACY ISSUE

What to expect in Obama's climate change speech, Shepard, Kate, Mother Jones Magazine, June 24, 2013.

CHAPTER 30 THE BUILDER

Personal communication, Tom Gorenflo Plum Island Construction website

CHAPTER 31 SEAWEED AND SAND DUNES

Galveston uses pesky seaweed to block storm surge. AP CBS, July 6, 2013. Just Seconds from the Ocean, Sargent, William, Lebanon NH, UPNE.com, 2008

Chapter 32 The Senator
Sand mining proposal progresses for residences. Hendrickson, Dyke, Newburyport Daily News, July 7, 2013.

Chapter 33 The MRBA
Tensions swell as beach erodes. Jim Rutenberg New York Times, June 27, 2013. State of the beach, MA Beaches, Beachapedia

Chapter 34 Siasconset
Just Seconds from the Ocean; Sargent, William, Lebanon NH. UPNE.com 2008. Siasconset Beach Preservation Foundation letter to the Nantucket Board of Selectmen.

Chapter 35 Raising Caine
Highlands officials propose raising entire town 11 feet in $200 million proposal. Penton, Kevin, Ashbury Park Press August 8, 2013.

Chapter 36 The Basin
Beach alliance pushes to secure funds. Hendrickson, Dyke, Newburyport Daily News, August 17, 2013.

Chapter 38 "Why That's Unconstitutional!"
Alberta government officials to buy houses in flood-prone areas. Cryderman, Kelly, The Alberta Globe Mail, August 22, 2013.

Chapter 39 The High Sandy Pachyderm
Was Plum Island home to ancient mammoths? Schwartz, David, Newsday, August 14, 2013. U.S moves ahead on plans to sell Plum Island, home of research laboratory. Rutenberg, Jim, New York Times, August 30, 2013. Long Island controversy spills over to Plum Island, Macone, John, Newburyport Daily News August 30, 2013.

Chapter 40 At an Ancient Orgy
Water temperatures bringing major changes. Newburyport Daily News editorial September 3, 2013.

Chapter 41 The Kartland Arms
Fill permit for Kartland development approved. Chiaramida, Angelijean, Newburyport Daily News, September 11, 2013.

Chapter 42 The Seaside Heights
NJ Boardwalk fire linked to Sandy damaged wiring. Parry, Wayne, AP September 17, 2013.

Chapter 43 Sandy's Silver Lining

The kindest cut of all. James, Will, Wall Street Journal February 18, 2013.

Chapter 44 Plum Island

Plum Island proposal brings dissent, Hendrickson, Dyke, Newburyport Daily News, October 1, 2013.

Chapter 45 Flood Insurance? Build an Ark!

Flood insurance rate increase hits hard in Florida, Gibson, William, Orlando Sentinel, September 28, 2013.

Chapter 46 Sewer Talk

Water sewer issues aired, condition of PI hydrants, connections a concern. Rogers, Dave, Newburyport Daily News October 17, 2013.

Chapter 47 Mike Morris

Personal communication.

Chapter 48 Flood Maps

Worries grow over impact of coastal flood policy, Hendrickson, Dyke, October 26, 2013.

Chapter 49 "Why Would I Want to Live in a War Zone?"

Mixed bag as communities continue Sandy recovery. Here and Now, NPR October 2013. Nearly a year after storm NJ uninsured, seasonal renters start to regain footing. O'Neill, Erin, New Jersey State –Ledger September 8, 2013.

Chapter 50 In the Belly of the Beast

Personal communication.

Chapter 51 Introducing Oysters

Cultivating the eastern oyster. Wallace, Richard, Southern Regional Aquaculture Center August 21, 2001

Chapter 52 The Deal

Newbury completes sale of biggest parcel on Plum Island, Solis, Jennifer, Newburyport Daily News, December 13, 2013. Marine complex in South Boston gets green light. Palmer, Thomas C. The Boston Globe September 12, 2007. On Nantucket Karp shadow looms over downtown. Tait, Shepard, Newburyport Daily News, October 17, 2007.

Chapter 53 The Stigma

"Stigma gives Plum Island homeowners a tax break, Hendrickson, Dyke, Newburyport Daily News, December 4, 2013.

Chapter 54 De Sinterklaastorm

Going with the flow. Kimmelman, Michael, New York Times February 13, 2013. New paradigm, living with water. Ambassador Renee Jones-Bos, keynote address, American Planning Association 2012. Extratropical cyclone Xaver moves slowly across Europe. Air Worldwide December 6, 2013.

Chapter 55 The Seawall

More sand eyed for battered beaches. Hendrickson, Dyke, Newburyport Daily News, February 17, 2013. The start of "sand wars." Daley, Beth, NE Center for Investigative Reporting, December 15, 2013.

Chapter 58 The New Year's Storm

Post-storm review finds Plum Island's rock walls held. Rogers, Dave, Newburyport News, January 6, 2014

Chapter 60 The Jetty

In Newbury, anger, frustration over Plum Island woes. Solis, Jennifer, Newburyport News, January 16, 2014. Jetty repairs to begin, Rogers, Dave, Newburyport News December 27, 2014.

Chapter 61 The Trifecta

Newbury officials very responsive to PI woes, Watt letter to the editor, Newburyport News January 21, 2014

Chapter 62 Filling in the Gaps

Help arrives for island landmark, Rogers, Dave, Newburyport News, January 20 2014

Chapter 62 The Trouble with Flood Insurance

Ron Barrett, personal communication.

Made in the USA
Middletown, DE
23 September 2016